ETHICAL IS
YOUTH V

D0601493

Ethical Issues in Youth Work presents a systematic analysis of some of the core ethical dilemmas facing youth workers in their day-to-day practice. Among the topics discussed are:

- when to break confidentiality
- the ethics of religious conversion
- conflicts between cultures
- balancing the autonomy and control of young people
- maintaining an equilibrium between accountability to funders, employers and young people.

This book also examines some of the key challenges facing youth workers in the context of public fears of youth crime, lawlessness, drug use, teenage pregnancy and policies designed to control and contain as well as educate and care for young people.

Ethical Issues in Youth Work offers a timely and unique insight into both the perennial dilemmas of youth work practice and some of the more recent challenges faced by youth workers in the light of current public attitudes and government policy towards young people.

Sarah Banks is Lecturer in Community and Youth Work at Durham University. She is the author of *Ethics and Values in Social Work* (1995).

PROFESSIONAL ETHICS
General editor: Ruth Chadwick
Centre for Professional Ethics, University of Central Lancashire

Professionalism is a subject of interest to academics, the general public and would-be professional groups. Traditional ideas of professions and professional conduct have been challenged by recent social, political and technological changes. One result has been the development for almost every profession of an ethical code of conduct which attempts to formalise its values and standards. These codes of conduct raise a number of questions about the status of a 'profession' and the consequent moral implications for behaviour.

This series seeks to examine these questions both critically and constructively. Individual volumes will consider issues relevant to particular professions, including nursing, genetic counselling, journalism, business, the food industry and law. Other volumes will address issues relevant to all professional groups such as the function and value of a code of ethics and the demand of confidentiality.

Also available in this series:

ETHICAL ISSUES IN YOUTH WORK

Edited by Sarah Banks

R Routledge
Taylor & Francis Group

LONDON AND NEW YORK

First published 1999
by Routledge
2 Park Square, Milton Park, Abingdon, Oxon, OX14 4RN

Simultaneously published in the USA and Canada
by Routledge
270 Madison Ave, New York, NY 10016

Reprinted 2003, 2004, 2006

Transferred to Digital Printing 2007

Routledge is an imprint of the Taylor & Francis Group, an informa business

Typeset in Times by Routledge
Printed and bound in Great Britain by
TJI Digital, Padstow, Cornwall

British Library Cataloguing in Publication Data
A catalogue record for this book is available from the British Library

Library of Congress Cataloging in Publication Data
A catalogue record for this book has been requested

ISBN10: 0–415–16500–8 (hbk)
ISBN10: 0–415–16501–6 (pbk)

ISBN13: 978–0–415–16500–6 (hbk)
ISBN13: 978–0–415–16501–3 (pbk)

CONTENTS

CONTENTS

Part II Ethical issues in practice 75

CONTRIBUTORS

Sarah Banks is Lecturer in Community and Youth Work at Durham University. Her publications in the field of professional ethics include *Ethics and Values in Social Work* (Macmillan 1995). She is currently writing a book on ethics and the changing social professions.

David Crimmens works in the social work department of the University of Lincolnshire and Humberside. Practice experience includes adventure playgrounds, detached youth work, intermediate treatment and residential childcare. Current research interests are focusing on rights and responsibilities in work with young people in Europe.

Maxine Green is one of two National Youth Officers for the Church of England. She is the coordinating moderator for the Eastern Regional Accreditation and Moderation Panel for Youth and Community Work and a member of the NCVYS training strategy group.

Umme F. Imam is Lecturer in Community and Youth Work at Durham University and a member of the editorial group of the journal *Youth and Policy*. She has written on the themes of work with black young people and domestic violence. Her current research is focusing on the coping strategies and needs of black children in relation to woman abuse and South Asian young women's experiences of violence and abuse.

Tony Jeffs is Senior Lecturer in Community and Youth Work at

Durham University. He has written extensively on youth policy and youth work and was a founding editor of *Youth and Policy* journal. He is currently undertaking research on the themes of informal and community education, including a book on Henry Morris and community schools.

Kenneth McCulloch is Senior Lecturer in Community Education at Moray House Institute, University of Edinburgh. After twenty years in local authority community education he continues to work with young people from time to time as a volunteer; his research interests are in the content and effects of youth work.

Phil Mizen teaches social policy in the Department of Applied Social Studies, at the University of Warwick. He has researched and published in the area of youth, unemployment and training, and is currently researching the lives of working children in Britain.

Sue Morgan is a youth worker with North Yorkshire County Council in Richmondshire. She has a particular interest in the use of counselling skills in youth work and the role of youth workers in child abuse and protection.

Mark Smith is Rank Research Fellow and Tutor at the YMCA George Williams College, London. He has published widely on youth work, youth issues and informal education.

Lyn Tett is Director of Community Education at Moray House Institute, University of Edinburgh. Her research interests are in the policy and practices that lead to active participation in educational decision-making by socially excluded groups and individuals.

Andy West is Research and Development Officer, Save the Children (UK). He has worked as a university lecturer, youth worker, welfare rights worker, and youth counsellor. He has researched and worked with vulnerable children and young people, including survivors of abuse, those who are homeless and, recently, street children in Bangladesh.

Anna Whalen works for Save the Children Fund in Hull. She is a youth and community worker who is currently coordinating a project with Kingston upon Hull Social Services and the Warren Centre for Young People, aimed at children and young people at risk.

Kerry Young is an independent consultant and part-time lecturer at De Montfort University, Leicester where she teaches on a range of young and community work courses. She has worked as a detached youth worker and also as a development officer and manager in a number of national youth work organisations.

SERIES EDITOR'S PREFACE

Professional Ethics is now acknowledged as a field of study in its own right. Much of its recent development has resulted from rethinking traditional medical ethics in the light of new moral problems arising out of advances in medical science and technology. Applied philosophers, ethicists and lawyers have devoted considerable energy to exploring the dilemmas emerging from modern health-care practices and their effects on the practitioner–patient relationship.

But the point can be generalised. Even in health care, ethical dilemmas are not confined to medical practitioners. And beyond health care, other groups are beginning to think critically about the kind of service they offer and about the nature of the relationship between provider and recipient. In many areas of life, social, political and technological changes have challenged traditional ideas of practice.

One visible sign of these developments has been the proliferation of codes of ethics, or of professional conduct. The drafting of such a code provides an opportunity for professionals to examine the nature and goals of their work, and offers information to others about what can be expected from them. If a code has a disciplinary function, it may even offer protection to members of the public.

But is the existence of such a code itself a criterion of a profession? What exactly is a profession? Can a group acquire professional status, and if so, how? Does the label 'professional' have implications, from a moral point of view, for acceptable behaviour, and if so how far do such implications extend?

The subject matter of this volume, youth work, does not have a code of ethics and is not, as the editor points out, readily identifiable as a profession in the sense that, say, medicine is. Sarah Banks points to differences of view among those involved in youth work, including a strand of anti-professionalism. And yet, as she says, there are issues arising in youth work which are analogous to those in those professions identified as the 'caring' ones. Banks says in her introduction that 'there is no doubt that youth work is in some kind of "quasi" [professional] category'. This volume makes a particularly interesting contribution to the series in that it both reflects on the boundaries of the category of 'profession' and discusses the practical issues facing those who are involved in youth work.

The Professional Ethics series seeks to examine ethical issues in the professions and related areas both critically and constructively. Individual volumes address issues relevant to all professional groups, such as the nature of a profession and the function and value of codes of ethics. Other volumes examine issues relevant to particular professions, including those which have hitherto received little attention, such as general practice, health care management and social work.

ACKNOWLEDGEMENTS

I would like to thank my colleague, Tony Jeffs, for offering advice, comments and enthusiastic support for this work on ethical issues in youth work. His sustained encouragement and interest have been invaluable. I am also grateful to several cohorts of Durham University community and youth work students for their willingness to share their ethical dilemmas and debate issues which have helped crystallise some of the thinking behind this book.

Part I

THE ETHICAL CONTEXT OF YOUTH WORK

1

ETHICS AND THE YOUTH WORKER

Sarah Banks

Introduction

> While out on a trip with a group of young people, a youth
> worker saw one of the participants, a young woman,
> stealing sweets from a shop. Nobody else seemed to have
> noticed. The young woman had recently returned to the
> youth club after a long absence and her behaviour was
> often challenging. The worker felt she was just beginning to
> develop a relationship of trust with the young woman, and
> therefore decided not to mention the theft. Afterwards the
> worker wondered if she had done the right thing, knowing
> that: 'by not mentioning the incident, I was condoning the
> theft and passing on the value that it was acceptable'.

All youth workers can give examples of similar incidents and
dilemmas – of cases where they have debated hard about what to
do, and wondered afterwards if what they did was right. Youth work
is full of ethical tensions and dilemmas. As one of the occupations
working within the welfare system it shares with social work,
nursing and medicine the classic dilemmas between respecting individual choice and promoting the public good; and between
empowering and controlling. Like social work, it has to work within
societal ambivalence towards its 'client group' (young people are
often regarded as threatening or undeserving) – balancing the roles
of carer, protector, advocate and liberator. Insofar as it is an occupation concerned with providing a service to clients, youth work
shares with a broad group of occupations commonly classed as
professions concerns about professional integrity, trustworthiness
and honesty in relation to its service users.

Yet little has been written specifically on ethics and youth work.

In part this is because little has been written on youth work generally. There are a number of explanations for this. Youth work is a relatively small occupational group; its occupational boundaries are somewhat blurred; the work is delivered through a variety of statutory and voluntary organisations; a large proportion of its workers are volunteers, with college-trained workers forming a tiny minority until recently; a significant feature of the work is a closeness to the young people being worked with; and there is a strong current of 'anti-intellectualism' and anti-professionalism in the work.

Nevertheless, youth workers are a significant group of people. It is estimated that there are 550,000 people engaged in youth work in the UK today, although the majority of these are part-timers and volunteers (National Youth Agency 1997a: 9). Concern about the 'problems' caused by and facing young people is as high as it ever has been – generating a concern about their moral education at school and at home, and demands for more overt control through mechanisms such as curfews or compulsory training. Youth work agencies are making claims for the role of youth work in reducing youth crime, drug-taking, teenage pregnancies and for enhancing sexual health and encouraging responsible citizenship. This makes it an opportune time to examine ethical issues in youth work.

In setting the scene for the rest of the book, this chapter will examine the nature of youth work and consider debates about the boundaries of the work and its status as a 'profession'. It will explore the ethics of youth work from two different perspectives. The first is a 'principle-based' approach which focuses on the core values and ethical principles said to underpin the work. These principles are about how workers should act towards young people – for example, that they should respect young people's rights, respect cultural diversity and work for participatory democracy. Many of the chapters in this book are about exploring further what such principles mean, how they can be implemented, and how different principles may conflict. A second perspective on ethics, virtue-based ethics, is then considered, where the focus is not on principles for action, but on the dispositions or character traits (for example, honesty, integrity, trustworthiness) that are integral to good youth work. Both approaches provide useful frameworks for examining ethical issues in youth work, although virtue ethics has been under-explored in the context of professional ethics.

Professional ethics and youth work

Professional ethics can be described in general terms as the study of the ethical issues arising in the context of people doing their work. It covers the special virtues required and obligations taken on by a person in a work role, how these virtues and obligations are defined and implemented, how conflicting obligations are handled and ethical judgements made. However, although the term 'profession' can be used loosely as a synonym for 'occupation', meaning a type of work or job, in the context of professional ethics it is usually used to refer to a subset of occupations which possess certain characteristics or about which certain claims are made. Exactly what these characteristics are has been the subject of a long debate (see Koehn 1994). Many theorists following the 'trait theory' have listed certain sets of characteristics as the defining features of a profession, such as: the existence of a professional association, a code of ethics, a system of qualification and controlled entry, state licensing of practitioners, and a specialist or esoteric body of knowledge (Greenwood 1957; Millerson 1964). The trait theory led to certain occupations, such as social work and nursing which do not possess the complete range of characteristics, being categorised as semi- or quasi-professions (Etzioni 1969). Other theorists have criticised this approach for failing to capture the essence of professionalism, which is largely about occupational groups making a claim to a certain status, which gives their members power over their work and in society generally (Johnson 1972; Hugman 1991).

Whether we adopt the trait approach or the status/power approach to professionalism, there is no doubt that youth work is in some kind of 'quasi' category. For not only does it not possess a professional association, code of ethics or state licence, but its practitioners are ambivalent about making any claims for professional status. This reflects the value placed by certain traditions within youth work on working alongside young people – whether as friend, ally, equal or enabler. Traditional models of professionalism which assume a distance between professional and client, with the practitioner as powerful expert, do not fit easily with these conceptions of the role of the youth worker. This applies as much to the . nineteenth-century idea of the youth worker as friend/guide (see Young's chapter in this volume) as to the radical conception of the worker as ally or fellow-campaigner.

However, it is not just youth workers' ambivalence about making claims for professional status that has made it difficult for those who have wanted to move in this direction. It is also the diverse and disparate nature of the work, and the difficulty in defining the youth work role. As with many of the welfare professions, a number of voluntary, independent and charitable organisations provide youth work, and a large number of volunteers deliver the work. The four examples in McCulloch and Tett's chapter give a good impression of the range of youth work agencies. Insofar as many of these organisations are at least partially funded from government sources, then they are part of the state-sponsored welfare system. As such they are subject to or influenced by national trends in thinking about the nature and purpose of youth work. However, there is also a large number of independent national and local voluntary organisations working with young people such as Scouts, Guides, Woodcraft Folk and some church organisations. These organisations tend to be included as part of the 'Youth Service', with the implication that they are offering youth work. Indeed, the uniformed organisations are included in the occupational and functional mapping exercise that has recently taken place for youth work (Brown and Draper 1997). Yet the people delivering the work on the ground would perhaps rarely identify themselves as 'youth workers'. They are volunteers working with young people who might go under the titles of 'Brown Owl' or 'Vicar'. Whilst the boundaries between public and private, professional and voluntary are fluid, they do need to be drawn if the notion of professional ethics is to make sense.

The boundaries of youth work

I have already located youth work as part of the 'welfare system'. It can be regarded as part of what we might still call the welfare state, in that a significant number of workers are employed by local authorities and/or funded by local and central government. Like social work, teaching, medicine and nursing, for example, youth work is partly about offering a free or subsidised service to a 'client group' deemed to be in need. Some of the ethical issues arising in the work, therefore, derive from the contradictory roles played by the welfare state professionals in caring for, socialising, controlling, helping and educating the people with whom they work. Such conflicts are not so apparent in professions like architecture, law, or accountancy, for example, where private practice is dominant and the client or customer is not categorised as sick, disadvantaged, ignorant or vulnerable. Ethical issues relating to public accountability, or conflicts between the client's needs and the public good, are much more evident in state-sponsored welfare work.

The definition of the work of an occupational group and the boundaries around it are always difficult to define. However, the lack of a professional association and the fact that the title of 'youth worker' is not legally protected (that is, anyone can call themselves a youth worker, regardless of qualifications and experience) means that this is particularly problematic in youth work. The work of Tucker (1994, 1997) suggests that youth workers are very unclear about their professional identity. Like the teacher, the youth worker is concerned with education, but not normally in a formal or compulsory context. Like the social worker, the youth worker has a caring and controlling role, but not in a legal context. As Mark Smith (1988: 53) comments:

> Workers may 'know' that they are not teachers or social workers but are unable to find enough in the concept of 'youth worker' to explain their role.

Part of the intangibility of the work is that definitions and statements of purpose usually focus on the process of the work, which has tended to be characterised as social or informal education. This is a very difficult concept to pin down. Recent work developing the concept of informal education (Smith 1988; Jeffs and Smith 1996) is helping to define the work more clearly. Smith (1988: 126–33) lists the key characteristics of informal education which include: the process is based on dialogue; it works with cultural forms that are familiar to participants; participation is voluntary; it takes place in a variety of settings; it has educational goals but these may not always be clearly specified; and it makes use of experiential as well as assimilative patterns of learning. It is important to note that education can be regarded as both a process (of learning, developing) and an end (a state of having learnt or developed).

So education is both the process and the purpose of youth work. But education is not neutral. How it turns out depends on what is learnt and how people develop. Paulo Freire, the Brazilian educator, spoke of education for liberation or for domestication (Freire 1972, 1997). His adult education and literacy programmes were about educating the poor and oppressed in order that they could understand and control their situations and liberate themselves from their poverty, their powerlessness and oppressive regimes. Education can also be for domestication, to encourage conformity, unquestioning

7

acceptance of the status quo, a form of controlling socialisation. Teachers, community development workers and youth workers may be involved in both these types of education. Somewhere between these two extremes lies what might be termed education for self-sufficiency – the enabling of individuals and groups to make their own choices and decisions within the limits of their social and economic situations. This is probably closer to what most educators are doing.

Other occupational groups in addition to youth workers also tend to use informal educational methods in their work and have education as their core purpose – for example, community workers, play workers, community arts workers or community education workers. Youth work has many commonalities with these types of work. Indeed, it is often the case that youth work is done by people who are also doing community work or informal adult education, and their job titles may be 'youth and community worker' or 'community educator'. What defines youth work is that it is informal educational work with *young* people. Other professionals working with young people (such as police, social workers, teachers) may also adopt informal educational approaches as part of their repertoire. But if informal education is not the main process used and the desire to provide an eduational experience is not the core purpose of the work, then they would tend not to be regarded as youth workers (see the chapter by Jeffs and Banks).

Nevertheless, defining the boundaries of the work is not easy. Those who are called youth workers may sometimes find that their main goals seem to be veering towards containment, conversion or control, if that is how their employer is defining the work, or that is what the funders demand. Whether youth workers *should* do such work is one of the ethical issues that arises in several of the chapters in this volume (see Green; Jeffs and Smith). How the question is answered relates to how youth work is defined, what are thought to be the core values of the work, and how these values are interpreted and implemented.

Several contributors quote the statement of purpose for the youth service produced following a series of ministerial conferences in the late 1980s and early 1990s (NYA 1990), which lists the core principles of youth work as: education, equality of opportunity, empowerment and participation. Interestingly the statement has been revised (NYA 1997b) and the terms 'empowerment' and 'participation' do not feature. However, even if these principles were universally accepted, there is still room for considerable debate about what they mean and how they can be put into practice. For example, there is a large difference between interpreting the empowerment of marginalised and socially excluded young people as funnelling them into a job, as opposed to working with them to explore a range of opportunities, to build confidence and make informed choices themselves (see chapters by Mizen; Crimmens and Whalen). Broad statements of purpose and principles give us something to discuss, but they do not provide the answer in themselves about how to act. However, it is worth looking at the values of youth work in more detail.

The values of youth work

'Values' is a much used word with a variety of meanings. In the context of professional ethics it tends to be used to mean the general ethical principles relating to how a practitioner should regard and treat other people and what counts as morally good and bad practice. Much of the literature on ethics in the welfare and caring field has tended to focus on the identification, interpretation and implementation of the core values or ethical principles of particular professions (for example, Bond 1993; Burnard and Chapman 1993; Horne 1987; Jones 1994; Tadd 1998; Timms 1983). The values are often discussed in the context of two different ethical traditions – Kantianism and utilitarianism (Banks 1995: 25–33). Kant, an eighteenth-century German philosopher, developed a theory of ethics based on the ultimate principle of respect for the individual person. 'Persons' are regarded as rational and self-determining – that is, capable of making choices and acting on them. Kantian ethics in a professional context tends to focus on respect for and promotion of the autonomy of the service user and would stress principles such as maintaining confidentiality, obtaining informed consent, not acting in a stigmatising or discriminatory manner or offering misleading or untruthful information. For Kant, any action which violated the principle of respect for persons would be morally wrong – regardless of whether it resulted in an outcome which could be regarded as beneficial. For example, if a youth worker lied to a threatening father about the whereabouts of his son, this would be regarded as wrong, regardless of the fact that the lie was told to protect the young man from being beaten up.

Utilitarianism, on the other hand, takes account of precisely such circumstances in its formulation of the basic ethical principle as the promotion of the greatest good of the greatest number of people. In the case of the youth worker above, the action might be regarded as morally right if, in weighing up the consequences of telling the truth or lying, the youth worker decided that more harm would be done if the truth were told. Utilitarian ethics judges the rightness and wrongness of an action according to its consequences. Core principles for professional workers relate to the promotion of the welfare of service users, the promotion of the greater good in society and the distribution of goods in a fair and just manner. Criticisms can be levelled at both Kantian and utilitarian systems of ethical thinking. However, for the purposes of this discussion it is sufficient to note that professional workers do seem to take account of both types of ethical principles in making decisions. Some of the most difficult choices and dilemmas relate to tensions between respecting individual freedom and rights, and the welfare of an individual or a larger group of people in society.

A useful starting point for looking at the values of youth work is the list published in the guidelines for the endorsement of quali-fying training (NYA 1997c: 6–7). These guidelines relate to training in 'youth and community work', which is the way most full-time youth workers in England and Wales are currently trained. The values underlying youth and community work are listed as follows:

1 respect for basic human rights – e.g. justice, freedom;
2 respect for the individual and rights to self-determination;
3 respect for the different cultures and religions in society;
4 a commitment to empowerment and participatory democracy;
5 collaborative working relationships and collective action; and
6 an acknowledgement that all relationships and activities with young people and adults are based on their consent.

As is often the case with such lists of values, this one contains a mixture of types and levels of statements. The first value – respect for basic human rights – seems to allude to the kinds of rights contained in international statements such as the United Nations conventions on human rights and the rights of the child – this would include rights to a fair trial, free speech, to adequate food and shelter, for example. These rights are very much linked to the second value: respect for the individual and rights to self-determination. Indeed, it could be said that the rights to justice and freedom (of which self-determination is a form) follow from respect for the individual. The sixth value about basing work with young people on their consent is simply an example of a more concrete and specific way of implementing the principle of respecting their rights to self-determination. So, these three values are all interlinked, with respect for the individual at the core. In philosophical terms, these could be categorised as Kantian principles based around the notion of 'respect for persons'.

The third and fourth principles are less about individuals and more about the kind of society we live in. Respecting different cultures and religions suggests that youth workers should value cultures and religions different to their own, not ridiculing or disregarding them, or trying to promote one at the expense of others. This might conflict with the principles relating to individual freedom, since cultures and religions are based on rules and doctrines which constrain people as well as contributing positively towards their identities. Interpretation of this principle could range from mere tolerance of alternative cultures, to a radical form of relativism which maintained that all cultures/religions are worthy of equal regard and status and we should not make judgements about them. The fourth principle about commitment to empowerment and participatory democracy could also be seen as linked to individual freedom and self-determination because it is about enabling people to have a say in decision-making (whether in a youth project or society more generally). It is unclear whether it refers to individual empowerment or collective empowerment. The latter would entail enabling young people as a group or 'class' to have a greater say in decision-making. Finally, collaborative working relationships and collective action are statements about the process of the work and the value placed on working together with colleagues and young people as a group.

These 'values' are very general, and in themselves tell us little about the ethics of youth work practice. They are broadly similar to the list of values for social workers (CCETSW 1995) and would probably be acceptable to most people working in the welfare professions. We rely, therefore, on discussion and debate of the type contained in the chapters in this book to elucidate the variety of interpretations of these values and look at what they mean in the context of youth work practice. Crimmens and Whalen, in articulating a rights-based approach to work with 'marginalised' young people, explore what 'respect for basic human rights' might mean in the context of professional work which takes this as its focus. It includes listening to young people; taking their views seriously;

giving them information; and involving them in decision-making about their lives. West's chapter on participative research adopts a similar position in relation to working with young people undertaking research on leaving care. He explores how young people can determine the design, execution and dissemination of a research project and how this raises dilemmas for workers who also want the research to be regarded as valid and credible. The principle of confidentiality is the subject of the chapter by Morgan and Banks. Confidentiality derives from the notion of respect for the individual and her/his right to self-determination (the right to decide what personal or private information should be revealed and to whom). Much of the discussion in the chapter is about circumstances in which confidentiality cannot be promised or must be broken.

In these chapters many more ethical issues arise than simply how to implement basic rights. The kinds of dilemmas that arise for workers relate to another set of key principles around the promotion of young people's welfare, including protection from harm by others or even by themselves. These can conflict with the basic rights connected with freedom and self-determination. In the chapters looking at the youth worker's control functions (Jeffs and Banks), and at funding for youth work (Jeffs and Smith), yet another set of principles is apparent in the work, namely the promotion of the public good, or public welfare. These may conflict with what is in young people's best interests as well as with young people's rights to self-determination. These chapters, along with that by McCulloch and Tett on accountability, also point up another site of conflict, that between a worker's values and those of a funder or employer. Chapters by Imam on work with young black people and Green on youth work in a Christian context raise complex issues around the youth worker's role and the extent to which they are mediators, interpreters, advocates or converters between cultures and religions. They starkly demonstrate the extent to which the bland principle 'respect for the different cultures and religions in society' needs seriously analysing and unpacking.

The National Youth Agency list of values is essentially premised on respect for individual rights alongside a respect for different cultures. The discussion above suggests that this is an incomplete list of ethical principles for professional youth work. Since a professional youth worker, working for an employer, usually has to promote other principles such as the welfare of the young person and the welfare of society in general. These are essentially utilitarian principles (linked to the idea of promoting the greatest good of the greatest number of people). In the chapter by Morgan and Banks, several examples are given of cases where agency policy requires a youth worker to break a young person's confidence, particularly in cases of suspected child abuse, in order to protect the young person and stop the potential abuse of others.

Another criticism could be made of the NYA list which entails a questioning of the idea that morality is based on a set of ethical principles relating to how people should act. This is exemplified in the chapter by Young, which, in addition to looking at the values of young people and youth workers concerning how they should act, also includes consideration of the kind of person a youth worker should be. She asks the question, what does it mean to be a virtuous youth worker? This is a different way of looking at ethics – from the point of view of the character of the agent or moral actor, rather than their actions or behaviour.

The virtues of the youth worker

In recent years in the field of philosophical ethics there has been a revival of what has been termed 'virtue ethics' (Crisp 1996; Crisp and Slote 1997; MacIntyre 1985; Slote 1992; Statman 1997). This is beginning to be covered in some of the texts on professional ethics (Beauchamp and Childress 1994; Rhodes 1986; Wilmot 1997), although it is often simply described as one of a number of ethical theories and not further developed in discussion of ethical dilemmas and decisions. Whilst there are many versions of virtue ethics, including that stemming from Aristotle, what they have in common is a focus on the character or dispositions of moral agents as opposed to abstract obligations, duties or principles for action. One of the reasons suggested for the growing popularity of virtue ethics is the failure of the attempts of Kantians and utilitarians to articulate sets of principles for right action. As Statman (1997: 6) comments:

> principles are just too abstract to provide helpful guidance in the complicated situations met in everyday ethics. These situations typically involve conflicting considerations, to which principle-ethics either offers no solution, or formu- lates higher order principles of preference, which, again, are too abstract and vague to offer any real help.

Virtue ethics is an approach 'according to which the basic judgements in ethics are judgements about character' (Statman 1997: 7). In Hursthouse's version of virtue ethics, an action is right if it is what a virtuous agent would do in the circumstances; a virtue is 'a character trait a human being needs to flourish or live well' (Hursthouse 1997: 229). What counts as 'living well' or 'flourishing' then becomes an important question in deciding what characteristics count as virtues. Some virtue theorists argue these vary according to different time periods and cultures (for example, the kinds of characteristics cultivated as virtues in ancient Greece may not all be applicable in twentieth-century Europe); others claim that there are universal virtues. Nevertheless, the kinds of dispositions usually regarded as virtues include courage, integrity, honesty, truthfulness, loyalty, wisdom and kindness, for example. A virtuous person will tell the truth, it would be argued, not because of some abstract principle stating 'you shall not lie', or because on this occasion telling the truth will produce a good result, but because that person does not want to be the sort of person who tells lies. Virtue ethics also tends to emphasise the particular relationships people have with each other. It could be argued that it makes more sense to see my kindness towards my best friend as arising out of the fact that I have a relationship of friendship with her, I like her and care about her, rather than from some abstract moral principle about promoting the welfare of others.

In relation to Young's chapter, and the role of youth workers as educators, then becoming a good person is not a matter of learning or applying principles, but of imitating some models (Statman 1997: 13). If youth workers are role models, then what are the virtues of the youth worker? In one sense, they should reflect the virtues recognised in society at large. According to MacIntyre the virtues are relative to culture and role; they are qualities 'the possession and exercise of which tends to enable us to achieve those goods which are internal to practices' (MacIntyre 1985: 191). While not all virtue theorists adopt this kind of view, the importance of roles and the idea of virtues as relative to 'practices' or communities of practitioners is a useful one if we are to attempt to articulate a virtue-based theory for professional ethics. We would have to ask ourselves what does it mean to be a 'good youth worker'? 'Good' would be internal to the role of youth worker and would be defined by the community of practitioners who do youth work.

Smith (1988: 106–23) briefly articulates a virtue-based ethics for youth work, seeing youth workers as educators whose role is to develop the 'civic courage and the other knowledge, attitudes and skills necessary' (ibid.: 114) to enhance human well-being – in particular to enable young people to pursue their own well-being or the 'good life' in the context of their local communities. Smith (1994: 165) explores youth workers' views of 'what makes for human flourishing – the good life' in relation to the importance of solidarity, cooperativeness and fostering a sense of community. Workers engage in this primarily through developing relationships with young people, central to which is conversation. This theme is further discussed in Jeffs and Smith (1996: 30) who suggest that conversation involves: concern; trust; respect; appreciation; affection; hope. Although not called such, these characteristics of conversation are more reminiscent of virtues than rules or principles. Jeffs and Smith (1996: 53) also emphasise the importance of what they call ' moral authority', which is about the workers having certain qualities such as being 'fair, truthful, punctilious about fulfilling obligations, thoughtful and unselfish in their conduct'. Workers will only be listened to if they are seen as trustworthy and deserving of respect, and if they practise what they preach.

To develop a full version of virtue ethics for youth work would require much more work. Indeed, it is debatable whether a virtue-based approach on its own could provide an adequate framework for professional ethics. Poole (1991) argues that a virtue-based ethics is not applicable in the public realm – the world of work. It can be applied to private or personal life where we do prioritise particular relationships and we may care for people because they are our friends. But the public realm is characterised by impartial market or justice-based relationships, often with strangers, where abstract and externally imposed universal rules and principles are important. Certainly the way in which professional ethics has been construed in recent years has been in terms of duties, rules and obligations relating to action.

To get a view of the kinds of virtues a professional worker might be expected to possess it could be instructive to examine codes of professional ethics, as these are partly about defining what type of person a professional is, as well as stating the ethical rules they should follow (Banks 1998). However, in examining codes of ethics in the caring professions (social work, nursing, counselling, occupational therapy, physiotherapy) the kinds of statements encountered all relate to the special obligations of the professional to act in a certain kind of way. Statements include: 'they will respect their clients as individuals' (BASW 1996: para 10); 'act always in such a manner as to promote and safeguard the interests and well-being of patients and clients' (UKCC 1992: para. 1); 'occupational therapists shall provide services to all clients in an equitable manner' (COT 1995: para. 3.2); 'counsellors must not exploit their clients financially, sexually, emotionally, or in any other way' (BAC 1993: para. B2.2.6). There is no code of ethics for youth work, but draft proposals are similarly action and obligation oriented, covering, for example: respecting confidential information, ensuring the safety of young people, maintaining high standards of professional conduct (Brunel University 1978; CYWU 1998).

However, in some of the codes of ethics for other professional groups, virtue-based statements are mixed in with statements of obligation. Here we find terms like 'honesty' and 'integrity' for example. Often the virtue terms appear in the form of an adjective. For example, the Royal Town Planning Institute code states that its members 'shall act with competence, honesty and integrity' and 'shall fearlessly and impartially exercise their independent professional judgement' (RTPI 1997: 1). The code for architects states that a member 'shall faithfully carry out his duties applying his knowledge and experience with efficiency and loyalty towards his client or employer' (RIBA 1997: 5). These kinds of statements relate to certain views about what it means to be a professional – namely, that a professional must be trustworthy, reliable, competent. A virtue ethicist would argue that it is less important that professionals claim to abide by explicit sets of rules stating that they will not exploit clients, that they will not discriminate on grounds of religion, gender, etc, than that they are particular types of people who have a disposition to act justly and fairly. They are fair, and therefore act fairly, not because of a rule devised by their professional association, but because being fair is part of what it means to be a good professional. However, this still leaves terms like 'fair', 'just', 'honest', 'competent' to be explored.

It could be argued that lists of virtues can be criticised in the same way as lists of values or ethical principles as being abstract and unhelpful in making everyday ethical decisions. It could also be argued that virtue ethics can be subsumed within principle-based ethics; that being a fair person simply consists in a disposition to act fairly. Therefore our moral judgements must be grounded in judgements about people's actions rather than their characters. This is an area that warrants much more discussion in the context of professional ethics. Recent attempts to develop an 'ethics of care', particularly in the field of nursing (Allmark 1995; Bowden 1997; Bradshaw 1996; Hanford 1994) are an interesting development of a form of virtue-based ethics, but remain unconvincing as a complete account of professional ethics for the reasons articulated by Poole and summarised above (see also Banks 1995: 34–5). We may conclude that an ethics of care that can take into account the particularity of each situation, people's relationships with each other, cooperation, communication and caring is important and complementary to an 'ethics of justice' which stresses universal principles, individual freedom, social contracts and duty. An over-emphasis in professional ethics on the latter may result in over-regulation, a damaging impartiality and neutrality and a mindless following of rules for their own sake. As Baier (1995: 48) comments, justice is found to be too 'cold' and 'it is "warmer" more communitarian virtues and social ideals that are being called in to supplement it'. Yet, at the same time, in the delivery of publicly funded and organised services, then universally applicable rules are an important part of what defines the work of the professional delivering these services. It is not expected that professional workers will give preferential treatment to their neighbour's daughter over and above a stranger, for example, although they might in everyday life. An ethics of care/virtue-based ethics and an ethics of justice/principle-based ethics are not mutually exclusive, but are, as Mendus argues 'complementary facets of any realistic account of morality' (Mendus 1993: 18).

Conclusion

In common with many of the other welfare professions, youth work has undergone a period of change in recent decades. More specialist roles for workers (see Banks and Jeffs) threaten the concept of a professional identity and shared values. A declining base in local authorities (Jeffs and Smith; McCulloch and Tett) means loyalties to a range of different interest groups and funders may conflict. A context when new policies for youth welfare and control are being introduced (Mizen; Jeffs and Banks) leads to the question as to the extent to which youth workers should be involved in work entailing compulsion and a stress on externally defined outcomes. None of these issues or conflicts is new, but together they are being experienced as an intense challenge. Against this backcloth, a call for greater clarity about professional values and ethics is being made (Banks 1996; Fairbairn 1997; Nicholls 1998). The debate about the need for a code of ethics for youth work, and a professional or regulatory body which was current in the 1970s (see Davies 1988) is now re-emerging. As one of the few explorations of some of the ethical issues in youth work, it is hoped that this volume will stimulate debate and a more detailed discussion of the issues raised.

Acknowledgements

I am grateful to Tony Jeffs for comments on an earlier draft of this chapter and to a youth worker for allowing me to use material relating to an ethical issue in her practice.

Bibliography

Allmark, P. (1995) 'Can there be an ethics of care?', *Journal of Medical Ethics* 21: 19–24.

Baier, A (1995) 'The need for more than justice' in V. Held (ed.) *Justice and Care: Essential Readings in Feminist Ethics*, Boulder, Colorado: Westview Press.

Banks, S. (1995) *Ethics and Values in Social Work*, Basingstoke: Macmillan.

—— (1996) 'Youth work, informal education and professionalisation: the issues in the 1990s', *Youth and Policy* 54: 13–25.

—— (1998) 'Codes of ethics and ethical conduct: a view from the caring professions', *Public Money and Management* January–March: 27–30.

Beauchamp, T. and Childress, J. (1994) *Principles of Biomedical Ethics*, New York: Oxford University Press.

Bond, T. (1993) *Standards and Ethics for Counselling in Action*, London: Sage.

Bowden, P. (1997) *Caring: Gender-Sensitive Ethics*, London: Routledge.

Bradshaw, A. (1996) 'Yes! There is an ethics of care: an answer for Peter Allmark', *Journal of Medical Ethics* 22: 8–12.

British Association for Counselling (1993) *Code of Ethics and Practice*, Rugby: BAC.

British Association of Social Workers (1996) *A Code of Ethics for Social Work*, Birmingham: BASW.

Brown, H. and Draper, M. (1997) *Occupational and Functional Mapping of Youth Work*, London: Department for Education and Employment.

Brunel University (1978) *A Professional Code of Ethics for Youth and Community Work: A Discussion Paper*, Uxbridge: Brunel University Regional Training Consultative Unit (Youth Services).

Burnard, P. and Chapman, C. (1993) *Professional and Ethical Issues in Nursing*, Harrow: Scutari Press.

Central Council for Education and Training in Social Work (1995) *Assuring Quality in the Diploma in Social Work – 1: Rules and Requirements for the DipSW*, London, CCETSW.

College of Occupational Therapists (1995) *Code of Ethics and Professional Conduct for Occupational Therapists*, London: COT.

ETHICS AND THE YOUTH WORKER

Community and Youth Workers' Union (1998) 'Your chance to speak up on ethics: Union consults on a code of ethics' *Rapport* March: 24–5

Crisp, R. (ed.) (1996) *How Should One Live?*, Oxford, Oxford University Press.

Crisp, R. and Slote, M. (1997) (eds) *Virtue Ethics*, Oxford: Oxford University Press.

Davies, B. (1988) 'Professionalism or Trade Unionism? The Search for a Collective Identity' in T. Jeffs and M. Smith (eds) *Welfare and Youth Work Practice*, Basingstoke: Macmillan.

Etzioni, A. (1969) *The Semi-Professions and their Organisation*, New York: Free Press.

Fairbairn, G. (1997) 'Is youth and community work morally aware?' *Ymlaen* (Magazine of Wales Youth Agency) 8: 8–9.

Freire, P. (1972) *Pedagogy of the Oppressed*, London: Penguin.

—— (1997) *Pedagogy of Hope. Reliving Pedagogy of the Oppressed*, New York: Continuum.

Greenwood, E. (1957) 'Attributes of a profession' *Social Work* 2(3): 44–55.

Hanford, L. (1994) 'Nursing and the concept of care: an appraisal of Noddings' theory' in G. Hunt (ed.) *Ethical Issues in Nursing*, London: Routledge.

Horne, M. (1987) *Values in Social Work*, Aldershot: Wildwood House.

Hugman, R. (1991) *Power in Caring Professions*, London: Macmillan.

Hursthouse, R. (1997) 'Virtue Theory and Abortion' in D. Statman (ed.) *Virtue Ethics: A Critical Reader*, Edinburgh: Edinburgh University Press.

Jeffs, T. and Smith, M. (1996) *Informal Education – Conversation, Democracy and Learning*, Derby: Education Now Publishing Co-operative.

Johnson, T. (1972) *Professions and Power*, London: Macmillan.

Jones, S. (1994) *Ethics in Midwifery*, London: Mosby.

Koehn, D. (1994) *The Ground of Professional Ethics*, London: Routledge.

MacIntyre, A. (1985) *After Virtue: A Study in Moral Theory*, London: Duckworth.

Mendus, S. (1993) 'Different voices, still lives: problems in the ethics of care', *Journal of Applied Philosophy* 10(1): 17–27.

Millerson, G. (1964) *The Qualifying Associations: A Study in Professionalisation*, London: Routledge and Kegan Paul.

National Youth Agency (1990) *Recommendations of 2nd Ministerial Conference of the Youth Service (England and Wales)*, Leicester: National Youth Agency.

—— (1997a) *Mapping the Youth Work Sector: A Summary Report*, Leicester: National Youth Agency.

—— (1997b) *Youth Service Statement of Purpose*, Leicester: National Youth Agency.

—— (1997c) *Professional Endorsement of Qualifying Training in Youth and Community Work*, Leicester: National Youth Agency.

Nicholls, D. (1998) *A code of professional ethics for youth and community work: a discussion paper*, Birmingham: Community and Youth Workers' Union.

Poole, R. (1991) *Morality and Modernity*, London: Routledge.

Rhodes, M. (1986) *Ethical Dilemmas in Social Work Practice*, Boston, Mass.: Routledge and Kegan Paul.

Royal Institute of British Architects (1997) *Code of Professional Conduct*, London: RIBA.

Royal Town Planning Institute (1997) *Code of Professional Conduct*, London: RTPI.

Slote, M. (1992) *From Morality to Virtue*, New York: Oxford University Press.

Smith, M. (1988) *Developing Youth Work*, Milton Keynes: Open University Press.

—— (1994) *Local Education,* Buckingham: Open University Press.

Statman (1997) 'Introduction to virtue ethics' in D. Statman (ed.) *Virtue Ethics: A Critical Reader*, Edinburgh: Edinburgh University Press.

Tadd, G. (1998) *Ethics and Values for Care Workers*, Oxford: Blackwell.

Timms, N. (1983) *Social Work Values: An Inquiry*, London: Routledge and Kegan Paul.

Tucker, S. (1994) 'Changing times, changing roles? an examination of contemporary youth and community work practice' *Youth and Policy* 46: 5–16.

—— (1997) 'Youth working: professional identities given, received or contested? in J. Roche and S. Tucker (eds) *Youth in Society*, London: Sage/Open University Press.

United Kingdom Central Council for Nursing, Midwifery and Health Visiting (1992) *Code of Professional Conduct*, London: UKCC.

Wilmot, S. (1997) *The Ethics of Community Care*, London: Cassell.

2

ETHICS IN AN AGE OF AUSTERITY

'Work–welfare' and the regulation of youth[1]

Phil Mizen

Introduction

This chapter is concerned with the ways in which welfare workers have been forced to confront a central ethical dilemma: how to reconcile the real benefits that state welfare provides with the requirement that those in receipt subject themselves to supervision and control. It does so by pointing to the ways in which this dilemma has become more acute in recent years as the form of state welfare has been subjected to considerable change. Although always bureaucratic, unwieldy and intrusive, workers could once point to the political commitment to social inclusion that underpinned the welfare state and the real improvements that followed. Now, it is argued here, such faith appears harder to justify as state welfare as a source of incorporation and concession has been discarded and new exclusive forms of provision have been put in its place.

As this chapter suggests, many welfare workers now find themselves in an increasingly difficult situation. Not only have they been forced to deal with the withdrawal of the state from its previous commitment to meeting needs, they have also had to face fundamental changes to the ways in which the state continues to discharge its remaining welfare functions. Whereas subjecting clients to supervision and control may once have seemed a price worth paying in exchange for an extended range of benefits, state welfare has more recently been directed towards a narrower set of criteria in which the reinforcement of the market is key. As this chapter points out, nowhere have these developments been clearer than in relation to the welfare of the young, as the state's active promotion of the market has underpinned the return to persistent and large-scale youth unemployment. Moreover, at a time when more and more young people have become reliant upon social welfare provision to meet their needs, the state has used this dependence to reinforce the power of the market over their lives.

The changing form of the state

The state has always sought to manage the tensions between production and the structural inequalities of market societies (Piven and Cloward 1971; Polyani 1957). In the immediate post-war period this reconciliation was attempted through a massive expansion of state activity centred on the public provision of welfare. In what became known as the welfare state, rising popular aspirations were harnessed to new forms of state activity directed at the public satisfaction of needs. Through the welfare state, the welfare of individuals was no longer to be left to the vagaries of the market, and its inability to provide for all, but was increasingly defined, prioritised and met according to a range of political and social criteria in which considerations of fairness, equality and the needs of individuals and their communities were paramount.

The expansion of state activity certainly produced a series of important improvements to the welfare of large numbers of people but brought with it a new set of dilemmas for the growing number of welfare workers. Not only was the effectiveness of these initiatives usually constrained by insufficient resources, indifferent quality and an often dubious set of objectives, but the form in which these benefits were provided facilitated new and more extensive modes of supervision and control. The expansion of the state took its influence deep into the social fabric and on into the lives of individuals and their families. Furthermore, in order to access the support and assistance on offer, recipients were required to endure an intrusive and degrading set of practices which, more often than not, actually worked to limit their freedom and curtail their capacity for independent action, rather than liberate them from need. As one set of commentators succinctly put it: 'it is true that the welfare state gives us some of the things we need, gives us "benefits", but it does so in a certain way, in a way that puts us down and oppresses us' (LEWRG 1980: 53).

Nevertheless, for a while this strategy of inclusion provided ready evidence of state welfare's progressive possibilities, as recipients and workers alike could point with conviction to the real benefits of an expanded welfare state. More recently, however, state welfare has been subjected to considerable change as previous forms of welfare have been dismantled and new ones erected in their place. Central to this process of restructuring has been the rejection of the previous emphasis on welfare as a source of incorporation, in favour of using new forms of state activity to regulate individual and social needs (Bonefeld *et al.* 1995; Clarke 1988). On the one hand, this has involved a redefinition of the boundaries between the 'public' and the 'private', as state responsibility for meeting needs has been curtailed. On the other hand, this process of change has also put in place new ways of organising the state's remaining welfare functions. Whereas state provision was once aimed at promoting social inclusion through concession, it has more recently been directed towards constraining popular aspirations within limits set by money and the market.

'Work–welfare' and the regulation of youth

The state has in recent years, therefore, pursued a restructuring process which has actually intensified the problems young people face. Its active subordination of welfare to the market has been expressed most vividly through the dramatic rises in unemployment over the last twenty-five years (Glynn 1991). Since the mid-1970s the priority successive governments have given to inflation and the creation of conditions conducive to business and investment has been at the expense of the more general need for a wage. The pursuit of sound money, reductions in public expenditure and the withdrawal of state support for industry have been felt largely through an ongoing restructuring of business activity and the intensification of work. The corresponding rise in unemployment has exposed young people's particular vulnerability to social and economic change, as job opportunities collapsed (Maguire and Maguire 1997). In a little over two decades young people's employment prospects have shifted from a relatively advantageous position – rates of unemployment among young people were actually lower than those of adults for much of the initial post-war period – to one of considerable disadvantage, as unemployment among 16–24 year olds has persisted at double the general rate.

It is difficult to underestimate the destructive impact of unemployment on the young and its disastrous consequences for their welfare (see Dennehy *et al.* 1997; Wilkinson 1994). The state's response, however, has been to use young people's greater reliance on public welfare provision to intensify this process of exclusion. Whereas welfare professionals could have previously looked to the state to provide a genuine degree of relief, this is now increasingly doubtful. Despite the rhetoric of a leaner, less interventionist state, state activity has intensified in unprecedented ways around a series of 'work–welfare' initiatives that have attempted to bind the welfare of the young more closely to the demands of employers (King 1995). Welfare professionals working with young people are now faced with an extensive network of measures, ranging from large-scale work experience and training programmes through to an increasingly restrictive social security system, whose primary purpose is to reconstitute young people's needs in line with the dictates of the market.

Training for work?

At the core of this restructuring process has been work experience and training programmes aimed at the young. School leavers in particular have been constituted as a category in need of special attention and since the early 1980s some seven million unemployed 16–17 year olds have been through government schemes. Moreover, in a parallel set of developments, the concern with school leavers has been extended to unemployed adults in general and those aged 18–24 years in particular. Through programmes such as the Youth Training Scheme (YTS), its successor Youth Training (YT) and sister initiatives such as Employment Training (ET) and Training for Work (TfW), the state has engaged in a wholesale programme of intervention directed towards reconstructing the young as a cheaper, more flexible and less demanding category of labour.

Thus, these schemes have been used to exert downward pressure on young people's wages. Rising youth wages have been held responsible for the erosion of young people's historical role as a source of cheap labour and for destroying the incentives for employers to take them on (Wells 1983). By paying trainees an allowance or 'top-ups' to their benefits and not a wage, the intention has been carefully to regulate young people's rates of pay and to force down their 'market' value. This cheapening of young people's labour has also been linked to the promotion of flexibility between occupational boundaries and the provision of low-grade generic skills (Pollert 1988). The aim has been to separate young workers from the idea that training involves the command of specific and identifiable skills tied to particular jobs through the promotion of training as a source of general work-related 'competencies'. Government training programmes for the young unemployed are 'not concerned with training for real skills in the traditional or craft sense. A few traineeships involve real skills training but most centre on experience in semi- or unskilled work' (Ainley 1988: 105; Mizen 1995). Indeed, the intention has been to use these as the basis for redefining young people's expectations of work by preparing them for a life of low-skilled, insecure work and for coping with intermittent spells of unemployment.

Young people's aspirations for work and quality training have also been progressively subordinated to the discipline of money, as training schemes have become ready targets for public expenditure cuts. Certainly programmes such as youth training have involved a massive injection of public funds but given their scale (at their peak around 450,000 unemployed school leavers could be found on government schemes) resources have always been tight. The introduction of the two-year youth training scheme was funded by only modest increases in expenditure and in the decade to 1993/4 real levels of public spending on government training and employment measures actually fell (McKie 1994). This has taken place despite persistently high levels of unemployment during the early 1990s and continuing shortages of skills. Pressures to curb public expenditure have also been realised through the creation of a national network of employer-led regional Training and Enterprise Councils (TECs) responsible for the delivery of training. With the introduction of TECs, training expenditure has been cut, real expenditure on each youth trainee has declined, the level of funding for adult programmes has been halved and employers have been unwilling to bridge the gap.

TECs have also been given the task of creating a national market in training to facilitate both the more efficient use of funds and a greater responsiveness to local labour market conditions (Peck 1991). The latter objective has, however, persistently come up against the insistence that the primary responsibility of TECs remains the delivery of government programmes. Attempts to create a training market have been similarly problematic. The provision of all unemployed 16–17 year olds with a Youth Credit to 'purchase' training has been unable to improve the quality of supply. The introduction of output related funding for TECs, whereby payment is linked to results (that is, a qualification or a job), has also reinforced young people's exclusion. Payment by results has encouraged training providers to select only those new recruits most likely to achieve a target outcome and, in doing so, has also further marginalised an already vulnerable group (Rolfe 1996).

Perhaps these developments would be less alarming if government training schemes had been more successful in revitalising the employment prospects of the young. However, it is doubtful whether these programmes have had anything other than a marginal impact on job chances and in some cases may even have been detrimental. The introduction of each new government scheme has involved the substitution and displacement of existing workers, as employers take advantage of subsidised labour (Finn 1987), and their status as low quality and remedial measures has often operated as a stigma (Mizen 1995). Graduates of government training schemes can also expect to receive significantly lower wages than those in other comparable groups (Bynner *et al.* 1997). Employers have also used programmes as 'shop windows', as ways of trying out new workers without guaranteeing employment or as a source of free labour. Even as unemployment levels have declined, employment rates have never risen much above 40 per cent and more recently only around one in four is going directly into work (Department for Education and Employment 1995).

From welfare to work?

The pressure on the young unemployed has also been intensified through the parallel restructuring of social security and employment service provision. The reconstitution of long-term unemployed young adults aged between 18 and 24 years old[2] into more uncompromising job-seekers, prepared to accept whatever work is going regardless of its suitability to their needs, has become a prime policy objective (Convery 1995; Morris and Llewellyn 1991). Long-term unemployment among young adults, in particular, is viewed as clear evidence of the ways in which the right to unconditional benefits has been responsible for the production of disincentives to work (Beenstock 1996). Rather than ensuring continuing contact with the labour market and rapid transitions back into work, social security has become equated with a 'dependency culture', in which continuing reliance on benefits erodes both the incentives to look for work and the skills, qualities and fortitude necessary to hold down a job.

Despite the fact that the bulk of the available research overwhelmingly supports the assertion that young people are desperate to work, the state's response has been to create a more punitive benefit regime designed both to increase the barriers to claiming and enforce welfare's deterrent effect. The real value of benefits has been steadily eroded, the entitlement of 16–17 year olds to income support has been replaced by the 'guarantee' of a place on a government scheme and lower rates have been introduced for those aged 18 to 24. Alongside this, the right to benefit has been progressively replaced by a greater emphasis on the responsibilities of claimants to take available work. The young unemployed are now required to demonstrate that they are both 'available for and actively seeking work' as a precondition for the receipt of benefit and must be able to muster proof if called upon to do so. The pressure to relinquish a benefits claim has also been increased by the introduction of the Jobseeker's Allowance (JSA) in 1996. Not only has the JSA introduced a lower rate of unemployment benefit for 18–24 year olds, bringing it into line with levels of income support, but all claimants are required to sign an agreement stipulating the precise steps being taken to find work (Finn 1998). Failure to comply with any of these requirements now risks invoking a more extensive range of sanctions.

The stricter benefits regime has also included the more intense assessment of a young claimant's continuing eligibility. For over a decade all unemployed people have been subjected to six-monthly Restart interviews, within which 18–24 years olds have once again been targeted as a priority group. Restart ensures a more methodical examination of job-search activities and a greater exposure to the full range of government schemes through the Restart 'menu'. Alongside this, concerted efforts have been made to reconstitute claimants' orientations to work through the introduction of mandatory re-motivation programmes, targeted specifically at the long-term young unemployed. Attendance at short counselling and guidance courses, such as Workwise and 1-2-1 Caseload interviews, is now compulsory. Their aim has been to limit the duration of benefit claims, scrutinise job-search activity and 'cool out' 'non-realistic' expectations of work. Like many of the other initiatives noted above, however, such measures seldom lead directly into work but have been more effective as a way of channelling the unemployed back into government schemes.

Ethics in an age of austerity

These developments not only compound the dilemmas faced by youth professionals, many of whom now find it problematic to manage the constraints imposed by 'work–welfare' with their clients' continuing aspirations for meaningful work and a living wage, they also pose a series of dilemmas regarding the capacity of youth work to sustain its traditions of autonomous, diverse and youth-centred action. Just as youth work was shaped by the expansion of the post-war welfare state, so too does this most recent phase of state restructuring have important consequences for its future.

This is because 'work–welfare' presents a direct challenge to many of youth work's most progressive practices. As Bernard Davies (1986) makes clear, youth work's emergence from its roots in the nineteenth century remoralisation movements was facilitated by its partial incorporation into more general post-war strategies of social inclusion. This did involve a strategic role in preparing young people for the demands of post-war citizenship. The access to large numbers of young people beyond the formal institutions of school and work, meant that youth work was well-placed to channel young people's increasingly conspicuous use of leisure time into 'healthier pursuits', dominated by considerations of hard work, moral responsibility and civic duty. Youth work could also help to regulate welfare capitalism's growing list of young casualties: the disaffected, unattached, destitute, homeless and criminal (see also France and Wiles 1997a; Smith 1988). Nevertheless, the new injection of resources provided an expanded and professionalised workforce, a modernised infrastructure and facilitated new and experimental ways of working with the young. The permissive legislative framework within which youth work operated, although withholding the security of statutory funding, allowed the tradition of voluntary and non-coercive association to survive, and in a few places even prosper. Unlike other comparable groups of welfare professionals, youth workers could point with some justification to relationships with clients built upon trust and mutual respect. The absence of a clearly defined curriculum and prescribed modes of working also represented an important alternative for large numbers of young people alienated by an increasingly formalised and extended period of compulsory schooling. Moreover, the continuing uncertainties over youth work's precise function facilitated a degree of latitude within which many workers could develop novel and challenging modes of practice. As Jeffs (1997) argues, it was within these

28

'spaces' that many of the distinctive, bold, experimental and some-times even radical innovations took place.

It is this tradition of independence and youth-centred provision that 'work–welfare' threatens, as the state seeks to reach out to new organisations to assist in its delivery and administration. Most immediately in a sector where budgets have been severely constrained, many youth organisations have been compelled into becoming more entrepreneurial. The need to find new sources of funding has been the major spur to the greater involvement of youth organisations in a series of initiatives, often well outside of their more familiar spheres of activity. France and Wiles (1997b), for example, have pointed to how many cash-strapped organisations have become involved in health education and crime reduction programmes. 'Work–welfare', with the considerable resources on offer, has also emerged as an important source of additional funding.

A number of organisations have managed to achieve some measure of reconciliation between 'work–welfare's' punitive thrust and youth work's emphasis on meeting the needs of the young. The payment to providers of training schemes or job-search and motivation programmes, for example, has encouraged some organi-sations to get involved in the planning and delivery of their own programmes. This has included the creation of a small number of training and guidance programmes that have gone some considerable way towards providing distinctive opportunities for work experience, skills and qualifications. Other organisations have also responded in creative ways by putting together distinctive training and support programmes for young people suffering specific hardships or strug-gling with particular needs. More subversively perhaps, there has also been space to redirect the resources from 'work–welfare' towards the support of core activities or to cross-subsidise other elements of pre-existing provision. Thus resources for 'work–welfare' have found their way into some genuinely original interventions, ranging from community and workshop skills and work experience projects, through to more specific interventions for those with histories of alcohol abuse, mental health problems and those living rough.

Some organisations have therefore responded to the dilemmas posed by 'work–welfare' in novel ways but its more general impact has not been so benign. Money does not come without strings attached and the sheer pressure of 'work–welfare's' influence threatens to submerge many of the distinctive and diverse traditions that youth workers have long championed. In exchange for these resources, involvement requires adherence to a tightly prescribed and clearly defined structure and content enforceable through contract and, more recently, by payment by results. Once involved the aims, objectives and often the actual content of individual elements of 'work–welfare' are developed within rigid and externally determined parameters, and subjected to regular and detailed scrutiny. Thus, for example, the non-placement or off-the-job elements of training programmes have been progressively marginalised in the name of employer flexibility and the ability of training providers to address young people's need for social education no longer has any meaningful presence. Even where the rudiments of social education remain, young people's exposure to what passes for social and life skills training has been constrained within a sanitised diet of basic numeracy, literacy and presentation skills, with little or no opportunity to provide a more expansive education.

These constraints further restrict the ability of participating organisations to remodel 'work–welfare' to suit their own specific agendas and the new funding arrangements have imposed greater limits on the possibilities of stepping outside of the original brief. The setting of targets and funding by results has been used to redefine the objectives of these programmes in line with a series of 'hard' or quantifiable outcomes: a qualification to NVQ level 2, a place on another scheme or programme, entry into further education or, less likely, a job. This has not only discouraged providers from taking on those young people least likely to achieve one of these 'outputs', it has also undermined their capacity to provide for the needs of those for whom such objectives are neither feasible nor desirable. It makes little sense, for example, to force an unemployed young person to make so many job applications each week, if they cannot make eye contact, hold together a conversation or are struggling with a history of drug abuse. Even for those young people unencumbered by such problems, the emphasis on 'hard' outcomes negates the considerable enthusiasm, energy and talents that many possess. Compelling a young person to join a training scheme or job motivation programme makes little sense when that young person has identified his or her own best interest as served elsewhere.

Thus 'work–welfare' also runs contrary to the stress that youth work has traditionally placed on retaining a youth-centred focus. The highly formalised structures, tightly defined content and specific objectives threaten to submerge youth work's voluntarism and informality under the weight of pre-existing programme requirements and arbitrary performance criteria. In doing so, youth workers risk being drawn into new sets of relationships in which they are required to exercise direct authority and control over clients. This has already happened to a considerable extent, as the structure of much of 'work–welfare' enforces a high degree of discipline, routine and compliance, ranging from the required weeks, days and hours of attendance to a stipulated mode of dress. Many youth workers therefore now find themselves placed in different roles, involving new social relations and new modes of conduct, centred on the containment, discipline and supervision of unemployed youth. These costs of non-compliance are high. For the organisation it means financial penalties, loss of funding and potential redundancies; and for young people the privation of no income.

Alienating the young

The involvement with 'work–welfare' therefore risks further cementing youth work's associations with a set of state practices that many view with suspicion and apprehension. This alone should be sufficient to alert youth workers to the need to rethink the nature of their involvement and the basis of the dilemmas it involves. Such a rethink has indeed been given a greater urgency by the election of a Labour government with an explicit commitment to tackling the exclusion of the young. The new administration's commitment to modernise the welfare state, create more effective routes from welfare back into work and put in place more responsive systems of support means that 'work–welfare' will continue to feature as a political priority. The promise of a systematic programme of support for the young long-term unemployed features as one of the new government's five central objectives and one which has been greeted with general enthusiasm. But as details of the 'New Deal' for the young long-term unemployed become clearer, rather than the radical break or clean sweep the initiatives epithet suggests, Labour's policies of 'tough love' look set to disappoint. Greater compulsion, stiffer benefit sanctions, an inflexible social security system, more training and work experience, low wages or 'benefit-plus' and little talk of real jobs are all too familiar themes.

If youth workers are not alarmed at the prospects of the 'New Deal' and its exacerbation of the current dilemmas they already face, then young people will view the prospect of yet another scheme with considerable misgivings. What can be asserted with a high degree of certainty is that most young people will not share the excitement or enthusiasm that exists in many quarters for Labour's

'New Deal'. Indeed, if it is to succeed in its stated objectives of meeting young people's needs for ways back into work, then it must face up to the reality of twenty years of accumulated deep-seated cynicism among those at whom it is aimed. This is not to suggest that unemployed young people are not interested in obtaining guidance and advice, or meaningful things to do. On the contrary, when asked, young people consistently articulate a desire for quality training and work experience provision and, most importantly, a realistic chance of a job with a living wage. They also want opportunities for guidance and advice.

It is, however, doubtful whether the 'New Deal' can overcome this deeply ingrained culture of hostility and misgiving. Few young people believe with any conviction that 'work–welfare' in general is sympathetic or useful to their needs, or that it can provide much in the way of genuine assistance (Murray 1996; Banks and Bryn Davies 1990). Indifference, suspicion and hostility pervades any scheme promoting compulsion and this ensures that participation is more motivated by the need to defend benefit entitlements than any positive endorsement. With the launch of each new scheme places have remained unfilled and compulsion has done little to overcome this; more young people just simply 'drop out'. At a time when the official unemployment claimant count is still well over one million, and with no other legitimate source of income beyond a training allowance, over 100,000 unemployed 16–17 year olds have chosen to simply drop out of the labour market altogether (Williamson 1997). Unemployed young people have long complained of the irrelevance of training schemes to their needs, the inappropriate nature of the work experience placements and of employers badly prepared to receive them. The suspicion that work experience placements are little more than exploitation, providing employers with 'cheap' or 'slave labour' runs deep and dissatisfaction with placements is rife (NACAB 1994; Banks and Bryn Davies 1990; Durning et al. 1990). Trainees may well appreciate the opportunity these schemes provide actually to do something in the context of few alternatives, but even these grudging acknowledgements are tempered by a sustained and deeply felt cynicism of the motives of both employers and government (Mizen 1995).

Young people have also demonstrated a remarkable propensity to act upon these feelings of grave distrust. Rates of early leaving from training schemes and guidance and counselling programmes are endemic (Durning et al. 1990; Training Agency 1990; Gray and King 1986), despite the severe financial penalties such action can invoke. Between one-half and two-thirds of all participants on government training schemes can be expected to leave early, and guidance and motivation programmes fare only slightly better. Early leaving rates among black trainees are even higher (Usher 1990), but for all trainees reasons for leaving are dominated by criticisms of their scheme's performances, doubts about the quality of training, the lack of advice or support and the paucity of the training allowance. While the single biggest reason for leaving is a job, it is a measure of 'work–welfare's' abject status among young people that the majority choose to leave for 'dead-end' jobs paying subsistence wages, in semi- and unskilled work.

Conclusion

Taken in sum, this expanding network of 'work–welfare' provision represents a far-reaching reorganisation of how the state relates to young people through its welfare activities. As a consequence, youth and other welfare professionals are now faced with a new and more intense set of dilemmas. Welfare workers have always had to contend with state welfare's contradictory status but the previous emphasis on accommodation and social inclusion made this appear easier to achieve. Most youth workers, however, continue to take this commitment to meeting young people's needs seriously, but this consistently comes up against the reality that this is not 'work–welfare's' primary concern. At a time when more and more young people have been forced to look to public welfare programmes for their livelihood and continued well-being, the state has responded through 'work–welfare' by attempting to reconstitute their aspirations more closely in line with the dictates of the market and within the limits set by money. In place of a commitment to work, the state now guarantees a place on a low cost, low wage, low skill, work experience or training programme. And where there was once the promise of a subsistence level of welfare benefits from the 'cradle to the grave', only punitive and supervisory forms of welfare provision now exist.

'Work–welfare's' growing influence on the nature of youth work provision has also compounded these dilemmas. While the state has continued to exercise an arm's length relationship to much youth work practice and provision, its influence is nevertheless being indirectly felt through the growing presence of 'work–welfare'. More precisely, in a sector always short of funds at the best of times, the relatively large amounts of resources on offer are proving difficult to resist. Yet these resources bring with them a different set of dilemmas which go right to the heart of youth work's continuing rationale. Unlike youth work's traditions of informal and self-directed participation, 'work–welfare' brings with it the prospect of a much more disciplinary set of constraints, and ones which young people themselves have not accepted lightly.

Notes

1 My thanks to Alan France, Sarah Banks, Mark Worrall and Pete Husbands of the London Connection for their help during the drafting of this chapter.
2 Approximately one in three of all those out of work for six months or more are aged between 18 and 24.

Bibliography

Ainley, P. (1988) *From School to YTS*, Milton Keynes: Open University Press.
Banks, M. and Bryn Davies, J. (1990) *Motivation, Unemployment and Employment Department Programmes*, London: Department of Employment, Research Paper No. 80.
Beenstock, M. (1996) 'Unemployment insurance without the state?' in A. Seldon (ed.) *Re-Privatising the Welfare State*, London: Institute for Economic Affairs.
Bonefeld, W., Brown, A. and Burnham, P. (1995) *A Major Crisis: The Politics of Economic Policy in Britain in the 1990s*, Dartmouth Press: Aldershot.
Bynner, J., Ferri, E. and Shepherd, P. (1997) *Twenty Something in the 1990s*, Aldershot: Ashgate.
Clarke, S. (1988) *Keynesianism, Monetarism and the Crisis of the State*, London: Edward Elgar.
Convery, P. (1995) 'Long-term unemployment declines', *Working Brief*, London: Unemployment Unit, No. 39.
Davies, B. (1986) *Threatening Youth*, Milton Keynes: Open University Press.
Dennehy, A., Smith, L. and Harker, P. (1997) *Not to be Ignored: Young People, Poverty and Health*, London: Child Poverty Action Group.
Department for Education and Employment (1995) *Youth Training Leavers Survey*, London: Department for Education and Employment.
Durning, J. M., Johnson, S. W., Shaw, J. L. and Lancer, P. (1990) *Efficiency Scrutiny: Take Up of Employment Department Programmes*, London: Employment Department.
Finn, D. (1987) *Training Without Jobs: New Deals and Broken Promises*, Basingstoke: Macmillan.

—— (1998) 'The stricter benefit regime and labour's new deal for the unemployed', *Social Policy Review* 10, London: Social Policy Association.

France, A. and Wiles, P. (1997a) 'Dangerous fortunes: social exclusion and youth work in late modernity', *Social Policy and Administration* 31(5): 59–78.

—— (1997b) 'The youth action scheme and the future of youth work', *Youth and Policy* 57: 1–16.

Glynn, S. (1991) *No Alternative? Unemployment in Britain*, London: Faber and Faber.

Gray, D. and King, S. (1986) *The Youth Training Scheme: The First Three Years*, Sheffield: Manpower Services Commission.

Jeffs, T. (1997) 'Youth work and the "underclass" theory' in R. Macdonald (ed.) *Youth, the 'Underclass' and Social Exclusion*, London: Routledge.

King, D. (1995) *Actively Seeking Work? The Politics of Unemployment and Welfare Policy in the United States and Great Britain*, Chicago: University of Chicago Press.

London Edinburgh Weekend Return Group (1980) *In and Against the State*, London: Pluto Press.

McKie, D. (1994) *The Guardian Political Almanac 1994/95*, London: Fourth Estate.

Maguire, M. and Maguire, S. (1997) 'Young people and the labour market', R. MacDonald (ed.) *Youth, the 'Underclass' and Social Exclusion*, London: Routledge.

Mizen, P. (1995) *Young People, Training and the State: In and Against the Training State*, London: Mansell.

Morris, L. and Llewellyn, T. (1991) *Social Security Provision for the Unemployed: A Report to the Social Security Advisory Committee*, London: HMSO, Research Paper No. 3.

Murray, I. (1996) 'Compulsion is not working', *Working Brief*, London: Unemployment Unit, No. 71.

NACAB (1994) *In Search of Work: CAB Evidence on Employment and Training Programmes for Unemployed People*, London: National Association of Citizen's Advice Bureaux.

Peck, J. (1991) 'Letting the market decide (with public money): Training and Enterprise Councils and the future of labour market programmes', *Critical Social Policy* 31(11): 4–17.

Piven, F. and Cloward, R. (1971) *Regulating the Poor*, New York: Random House.

Pollert, A. (1988) 'The "flexible firm": fact or fiction', *Work, Employment and Society* 2(3): 281–316.

Polyani, K. (1957) *The Great Transformation: The Political and Economic Origins of Our Time*, London: Beacon Press.

Rolfe, H. (1996) *The Effectiveness of TECs in Achieving Jobs or Qualifications for Disadvantaged Groups*, London: HMSO.

Smith, M. (1988) *Developing Youth Work*, London: Macmillan.

Training Agency (1990) *Two Year YTS Leavers 100 Percent Follow Up Survey*, Sheffield: Training Agency.

Usher, G. (1990) 'Employment Training: Britain's New Bantustans', *Race and Class* 32, 1: 45–56.

Wells, W. (1983) *The Relative Pay and Employment of Young People*, London: Department of Employment, Research Paper No. 42.

Wilkinson, J. (1994) *Unfair Shares? The Effect of Widening Income Differences on the Welfare of the Young*, London: Barnardos.

Williamson, H. (1997) 'Status Zer0 youth and the "Underclass": some consideration' in R. Macdonald (ed.), *Youth, The 'Underclass' and Social Exclusion*, London: Routledge.

3

PROFESSIONAL ETHICS, ACCOUNTABILITY AND THE ORGANISATIONAL CONTEXT OF YOUTH WORK

Kenneth McCulloch and Lyn Tett

Introduction

In this chapter we examine the ways in which workers, managers and organisations interact to facilitate or impede ethical practice in youth work. We use hypothetical case studies to illustrate how youth workers' understanding of their own role, and the expectations others have of them, will frame the context within which problems are both set and solved. We explore the organisational settings within which youth workers operate, in order to support a theoretical framework that illustrates the ways in which organisational size and culture can lead to differing conceptions of professionalism, accountability and ethical practice.

Professional and *professionalism* are not simply neutral, descriptive terms but are value laden and strongly contested. Wilding's (1982) critique represents professions as controlling and legitimising structures, operating in the interests of members of the particular professional group. Alternatively, professionalism can be understood as representing 'competence and [a] collective service ideal' (Airaksinen 1994: 1). We use the term professionalism in Friedson's (1986) sense, referring to a set of occupational practices, and by extension attitudes and beliefs. These practices, attitudes and beliefs form the common bond for a community of practitioners who also share a body of knowledge. However, neither the particular knowledge, nor the practices which spring from that knowledge, are fixed and unchanging. Recognition of the dynamic nature of the relationship between these elements is vital to an understanding of professionalism in youth work.

As Holdsworth (1994: 43) points out 'the professional has knowledge which other people do not have' and so is accountable to the rest of society for the ways in which such knowledge is used. Moreover, acting as a professional requires an attitude and approach that has to incorporate critical thinking and reflective practice. We believe that the diversity of youth work practice, which includes the volunteer giving a few hours to youth work as well as those who make it a full-time vocation, is encompassed in such a definition. The idea of professional*ism* follows from that, as a set of attitudes and practices to which any youth worker may aspire, whatever their level of training and qualifications.

Accountability necessarily has to take account of the guiding principles of a profession and involves judgement in synthesising conflicting objectives and values. However, a key characteristic of accountability is the willingness to lay 'oneself open to criticism' (Holdsworth 1994) from both service users and the public at large. This involves accepting responsibility for providing the fullest and most open account of our activities so that others may make judgements about our actions. Accountability also involves considering to whom workers are answerable – the profession, the organisation, the service users/young people, their own conscience. Conflicting accountabilities often present workers with their most acute dilemmas about what constitutes ethical practice.

By ethical practice we mean action that leads to human wellbeing from a perspective that values the disposition to act truly and justly. As Smith (1994: 76) points out, ethical practice 'entails an orientation to "good" or "right" rather than "correct" action...and allows people to break a rule or convention if they judge that to follow it would not promote "the good"'. At the heart of such practice is the principle of respect for persons which 'relates to other principles such as autonomy, non-maleficence, beneficence, equity and justice' (Henry 1994: 146).

Professionalism and accountability

The relationship between professionalism and professional values on the one hand, and organisational imperatives and accountability to an employer on the other, is a central issue for youth workers. The report of the Cullen enquiry (Scottish Office 1996) has led to increasing attention being paid to who is properly entitled to the label of youth worker, and to 'means of protecting children and young people who attend clubs or other groups against abuse by leaders or others who have regular contact with them' (ibid.: 139). Our central concerns are with how professionalism is conceived, and how differing organisational contexts for youth work can both influence the ways in which professionalism is understood and constrain or direct workers' beliefs and activities. As Jackson (1994: 122–3) points out, since practice always takes place in a specific environment, it is difficult to conceive of a common set of standards that would be espoused and interpreted in exactly the same way by the entire membership of a profession.

Youth work embodies a number of different traditions, each with its distinctive value stances and notions of purpose which are manifested in varied styles of work and attitudes to such matters as training or payment for being a youth worker. Smith (1988: 57) identifies specific traditions related to historical origin and differences of purpose. A key dimension of this model is the attention given to distinguishing 'professionalised' youth work both from the voluntary traditions of 'organic' small-scale neighbourhood-based work and from the 'movement traditions' represented by the Scouts, Boys Brigade, religious groups and political youth groups. There are elements in all these traditions that are in some degree convergent, such as an increasing emphasis on training and on what might be characterised as socially responsible or ethical practice. The fact that these trends operate right across the field tends to validate the broader notion of professionalism in youth work which we have proposed. By way of illustration, it is the Scout Association that is being widely recognised as operating one of the most sophisticated systems in the UK for identifying the suitability of persons volunteering their services as unpaid youth workers.

A number of authors (for example, Bloxham and Heathfield 1995; Smith 1994) have argued that the ability of practitioners to plan, reflect, analyse, manage and develop requires them to have a critical understanding of what they are doing and where it fits into the overall aims of their work. The ways in which problems are set and solved, however, will be constrained by what is viewed as possible and the forms of activity that are engaged in. How experience is labelled and organised determines how 'sense' will be made of particular events and in any profession this 'framing' (Goffman 1975) will determine what is seen and heard, and thus constrain the domain in which practitioners can change their practice.

Youth workers have traditionally had considerably greater autonomy in determining their work priorities than is common in other professions such as teaching and social work (see Smith 1988), but this also means that the underpinning beliefs, values and norms about what is appropriate practice may not be subject to much day-to-day challenge. What is judged to be 'good practice' will arise out of particular historical traditions and reflect a commitment to an elaborate, if not wholly explicit, set of beliefs. Where choices are made in a context where ends are not determinate and value conflicts exist about both ends and means, then judgement is crucial and will be guided by each individual's 'theory in use' (Argyris and Schon 1974). If youth workers are to explore their experiences and ethical accountability they therefore need to become aware of what the prevailing norms and 'common sense' views implicit in their practice are regarding practising what is preached. As Henry points out:

> professional accountability is central to the setting of standards and norms, and persons within the organisation are responsible for planning and managing the quality and delivery of the service, both individually and collectively. From a professional perspective there is personal and collective accountability for establishing and maintaining the standards of practice.
>
> (Henry 1994: 145)

Another important consideration is the way in which workers are held to be accountable to their organisations for the work that they do. Different conceptions of purpose are likely to result in different emphases on what is measured, whether these be processes, outputs, or inputs. This can also lead to a tendency to prioritise what is easily measurable. For example, a small local youth club would be likely to rate its financial independence and ability to recruit voluntary leaders as key measures of success whilst an organisation such as Barnardo's or Save the Children might place emphasis on the extent to which vulnerable young people were enabled to remain in their own locality rather than being taken into some kind of residential care. For many organisations externally imposed 'performance indicators' are used to assess the quality of the service that is delivered but a complex service such as that provided by youth workers can be difficult to measure (see McCulloch and Tett 1995). In local authority settings, youth workers' concerns for acting in what they regard as the interests of the young people around issues such as sexual health might conflict with a council's cautious policy. This also illustrates how concern for ethical practice can lead to conflicts that result in people breaking rules that are seen to be concerned with 'correct' rather than 'right' action.

One context in which conflicts around professionalism and accountability are most likely to arise is when different organisations, or different professions within the same organisation, collaborate. Collaboration is often difficult because it requires a change in approach that seeks to minimise differences in aims, culture and procedures between people that have different traditions of work. Milburn (1994) has suggested that much collaboration is 'phantom' because different workers and different organisations continue to work in parallel rather than by changing practices. 'True' collaboration would lead to 'collaborative advantage' (Huxham 1996) where something unusually creative is produced that is more than the sum of the contributing parts and can lead to some benefit for wider society that is beyond the remit of any of the participating organisations themselves. Creating open and sound working relationships will lead to 'true' collaboration. However, misunderstandings, antagonism, differences in values and differential expectations from the host organisations in relation to the accountability and availability of staff can seriously affect collaborative work. Interestingly, it is often only in collaboration with other professions that youth workers may become aware of their underlying professional values when they find themselves challenged to justify particular ways of acting.

Collaboration between different youth work organisations may throw up similar conflicts as the case studies below illustrate. An independent youth project may feel railroaded into taking particular action by the local council because it provides a large proportion of its income. From the project's perspective they are certainly not engaging in 'true' collaboration that would result in mutually agreed action. Similarly volunteers may have very different views about the purposes of their club from paid staff and so working together on a project that had shared aims and objectives can be problematic. Collaborative practice can lead to many advantages for organisations such as the more effective use of resources and skills, enhanced creativity, improved services for young people and increased staff confidence but it takes time and effort and an awareness of the context to enable effective work to take place.

The examples which follow illustrate some of the different organisational contexts in which youth work may take place. The case studies serve to characterise some of the different approaches and emphases that workers may experience across a range of organisational contexts in which youth work may be located and are designed to illustrate some features that may be found in settings of the general type described. They are hypothetical or 'imaginary', although their construction has drawn on real examples. The case studies also provide the basis for discussion of the influence of differing organisational perspectives on what is seen as ethical practice. Those questions are explored in the subsequent section.

The local 'voluntary' youth club

The Riverside Youth Club serves a long-established neighbourhood in a medium-sized town. In the late 1960s a group of local parents began with the aim of providing 'worthwhile activities' for local teenagers. Over time there has been a range of volunteers helping to run the club and no one has ever been paid for being a youth worker there. The club is managed by a committee of local parents and others and their first priority has always been to maintain independence and so offers from the youth service of participation in youth forums, training events and policy consultations have been treated with little enthusiasm.

The club meets for two evenings each week in the local school and the programme consists mainly of games and activities which change according to young people's interests and those of the volunteer workers of the day. Until quite recently, common sense was seen as the guiding principle and cardinal virtue. However, moves towards the accreditation of youth groups along with public anticipation of the vetting of adults involved in youth work have resulted in a significant shift in attitude. Club volunteers frequently discuss what they do, how they do it and how that might be perceived by parents and other outsiders.

The small independent project

Woodhouse Youth Project is based in a large council estate on the periphery of a city of about 450,000 inhabitants. Initially resourced through urban programme funding, it now operates as an independent organisation, but is substantially dependent on the city council since 70 per cent of costs are met by a council grant. The project management committee consists of local councillors, council officials and community representatives. The project runs a mixed programme of 'open' youth clubs for teenagers, a children's club and groups for young people referred to the project as 'at risk'. The latter are identified through the local social work team and local schools. There are five full-time staff in the centre, of whom three are qualified in youth work or community education, a fourth is a qualified social worker and the fifth has a degree but no professional qualification, having been appointed on the basis of extensive experience of working with young people in a part-time worker role. There are five paid part-time youth workers in the project as well as a variable number of volunteer workers.

The city council has adopted a joint strategy in relation to young people at risk of requiring residential care. The strategy brings together both the departments – Education and Social Services – with an interest in services for young people to carry out joint assessment and to develop and support projects which will help young people remain in their locality whenever possible. Alongside this, the council is replacing grant aid with service agreements, requiring a specific range of outcomes from contracting organisations, and with explicit measures of performance applied in evaluation of the service.

The national voluntary organisation

In 1988 the Homeless Children's Society changed its name and is now known as Youth Welfare UK (YWUK). From its foundation in the 1890s up to the mid-1960s the society's main activity was the operation of residential care homes and centres for city children in countryside locations. During the 1970s and 1980s the emphasis shifted away from residential care towards community-based programmes with objectives characterised variously as, for example, to prevent 'unnecessary' referrals to residential care, to divert young people away from crime, or to reduce or prevent drug use among young people.

YWUK is relatively secure in financial terms which allows the organisation to maintain a high degree of independence in its policy and practice. Typically, local projects or programmes would have three or four full-time staff and would be supervised by a regional officer; each of the five regional officers carry supervisory responsibility for up to ten projects. The detailed arrangements for the management of individual projects vary in a number of ways. First, the different level and nature of community involvement in management committees; second, the involvement of external funders varies ranging from projects entirely funded from the organisation's own resources to service contracts under which YWUK operates a service on behalf of a local council. Of the 127 project staff now in post, over half are qualified youth workers, with the remainder roughly split between those with teaching or social work qualifications. The overall gender balance is now weighted slightly towards women, although among project leaders 60 per cent are male. Seventeen staff identify themselves as black or Asian; of these, six are employed in two specialist projects working with black young people.

The local authority

Hillshire Council in North Central Scotland came into being when the former Regional Council was disaggregated to form five new single-tier authorities. The former council had a strong commitment to the provision of informal education programmes for young people through its Community Education Service. Hillshire Council decided to amalgamate its Community Education Service with the Library Service and the Sports and Recreation Department; the new organisation is called Hillshire Community Services Division (CSD) and lies within the responsibility of the Education Directorate but is administratively quite separate from the Education Division and its concern with schools. The authority serves an area of some 320 square miles and a population of 370,000. There are two main towns, seven villages of various sizes and a number of smaller settlements. The staff of the CSD are organised in five geographical teams each consisting of a mix of community educators, librarians and sports centre staff. Management operates in a strongly hierarchical fashion, decisions and policies being 'passed down' from above.

A current debate among staff concerned with informal work with young people is that around concerns with sexuality. Most of the community educators express an interest in working with young people on issues such as sexual and gender identity, sexual health and related issues. For some of their colleagues with a sports background, and for the library staff, many of whom are interested in youth work perspectives, this is very much unexplored territory. The (Labour controlled) council is cautious, even 'conservative', in its approach. In developing a policy for this work the council is seeking to impose a restrictive and fairly inflexible framework requiring advance parental consent to participation in sessions, and restrictions on what can be said about gay sexuality, which one worker characterises as 'effectively preventing us from talking about the issue at all'.

The organisational context: structure and culture

In general our focus is more on culture and processes than structural factors such as organisational systems. However, in respect of structure, Mintzberg's (1979) distinction between *machine bureaucracy* as a description of the classical hierarchical organisation, and *professional bureaucracy* is particularly helpful. The latter describes an organisational form which, while demonstrating many of the positive qualities of bureaucracy in respect of clear procedures, lines of communication and accountability, also incorporates a recognition of the legitimacy of professional autonomy. Such a setting might well be a reasonably congenial home for youth workers, and the concept of *professional bureaucracy* could reasonably be applied to some medium and larger voluntary organisations, and perhaps to some more enlightened local authorities.

The notion of organisational culture is somewhat problematic. However, for our purposes, we will use the definition offered by Bloor and Dawson:

> Organisational culture is defined here as a patterned system of perceptions, meanings and beliefs about the organisation which facilitates sense-making amongst a group of people sharing common experiences and guides individual behaviour at work.
>
> (Bloor and Dawson 1994: 276)

These authors offer a useful model for the interpretation of professional cultures and subcultures in their organisational context, emphasising the importance of 'patterns of signification, legitimation and domination' (Giddens, cited in Bloor and Dawson 1994: 278). The example of medical dominance over partner professions such as physiotherapy and social work offers a useful parallel with our hypothetical local government organisation of Hillshire Council. In this context the dominance of the teaching profession within education departments may influence the ways in which issues are framed and the imperatives which influence professional decision-making. Similarly, youth workers practising in a context where there is a statutory social work dimension to the relationship with young people may find their concerns and priorities subjugated to those of their social work colleagues.

Millar has argued that many youth services operate in a 'person' culture, in which the needs and desires of individuals within the organisation take precedence over the demands of the organisation itself and this orientation can lead to an oppositional stance to authority. She also points out that such services operate 'within particularly complex decision-making structures, where advisory bodies, management committees, inter-disciplinary steering groups all have a role in the process in addition to relevant local authority committees' (Millar 1995: 51). While we would challenge her characterisation of the culture of youth work as based on a somewhat oversimplified conceptualisation of organisational culture, we would agree that it can lead to a view of management as inherently problematic since in many of its manifestations it will be seen as antithetical to the dominant value-base that defines youth workers' professionalism. Banks (1996: 18) has summarised the principles underpinning youth work practice as 'informal education; equality of opportunity; participation; empowerment'. This can mean that activist youth workers may see managers as part of a structure of social authority that is oppressing the very people for whom they are seeking to establish equality of opportunity.

Workers experience the organisations within which they function as influencing their activities in many different ways. Organisations may impose rules or rely on workers' judgements; they may encourage or stifle innovation at the grass roots; they control resources such as time, money or equipment. The smallest and largest organisations may behave in similar ways in this latter respect even though the resource concerned might range from a five- or six-figure sum of money to control over the keys to the Scout Hut. Such tensions between organisational imperatives and the value positions that influence youth workers' purposes and behaviour lead us on to consider the concept of 'ethical climate' in organisations.

The organisational context: four 'climates' of ethical practice

The concept of work climate is chosen to represent a sense of 'how it feels to work here' in terms of the range of conditions for professional practice that may be encountered by youth workers. Victor and Cullen (1988: 101) characterise work climate in the ethical sense as 'the prevailing perceptions of typical organisational practices and procedures that have ethical content'. From an organisational point of view this is represented as the way in which individuals perceive their activities and autonomy as being more or less *pre*scribed, *pro*scribed or requiring permission. One example given is the way in which recruitment and selection decisions are conducted and understood. In our case studies, Riverside Youth Club and YWUK may well respond differently to concerns about equal opportunity in the ways they recruit and select staff.

Victor and Cullen offer a typology of ethical work climates using 'locus of analysis' and 'ethical criterion' as the key dimensions. 'Locus of analysis' refers to the source of ethical reasoning and leads us towards the importance of professionalism or 'community of practice' in the sense rehearsed earlier. 'Ethical criterion' differentiates the interests (self interest, joint interest or principle) that are dominant and is drawn from the field of moral philosophy. We have moved from this typology to develop the framework represented as Figure 3.1 where our first key dimension is accountability and different understandings of the 'professional'. The second dimension represents the ethical criterion manifest in the organisational priority given to right action or conversely to such criteria as public image. Like many such typologies it is somewhat simplified since the dimensions proposed represent complex concepts which are here reduced to bipolar constructs.

Figure 3.1 Organisational climates for professional practice

We suggest that accountability may be conceived in terms of control by the organisation or, by contrast, by reference to a professional ideal or ethic, and this polarity provides one dimension of our framework premised on competing representations of the professional – *the trained practitioner* and *reflective professional* ideals. The second dimension is represented as concern with organisational integrity and reputation versus concern for 'the good'. The two axes are not however of precisely equal significance. The accountability dimension is stronger simply because the effects of organisational priority on practice will tend to be less influential where practice ethics are derived from professionalism rather than from an organisational prescription. This framework enables us to conceptualise the climates of organisations in what we have chosen to describe as bureaucratic, parental–ethical, regulatory–ethical and professional–ethical approaches to ethical practice.

Bureaucratic

Originally conceptualised as a way of describing an ideal form of organisation for complex tasks, the classical bureaucracy (Weber 1947) is characterised by well-defined lines of communication and accountability, clearly defined job boundaries and distinct levels of authority to make decisions. The scope for autonomous action is limited and professionalism therefore becomes problematic in the sense that the organisation's imperatives are ascribed a superordinate or at least equal standing with professional codes. Consideration of the occupations characterised by Etzioni (1969) as 'semi-professions', for example, social work and nursing, reveal activities which are characteristically quite highly supervised and more often than not operate within a framework of bureaucratic hierarchy such as a local government administration or a hospital.

In the Hillshire case study it would be no surprise to find that youth workers experienced it as a constraining bureaucracy, concerned primarily to achieve corporate objectives and avoid criticism, and expecting professional staff to pursue the corporate purpose and to account for their actions within that framework. It may not, however, be the case that bureaucracy is entirely inimical to youth workers. One might argue that clear organisational guidance about what is and is not desirable or permissible in practice may well help workers to clarify objectives and to routinise a range of decisions that would otherwise take up resources of time and energy. Conversely, an organisational context that tends to deny or stifle professional autonomy might be more likely to lead to the atrophy of the ethical sense and to a loss of the capacity, by workers, to make their own professional judgements and to have confidence in their capacity to do so.

There seems to us to be a tendency for larger, more diversified organisations to be less respectful of the professional autonomy to which youth workers might believe themselves entitled. Hillshire Council has organised its services in such a way that the work of youth workers is not necessarily supervised by professional peers (although it may be) and the autonomy of workers to follow their own judgements, or even to adopt a distinctive stance on an issue such as work with young people on sexuality issues, is severely constrained. By contrast, the experience of YWUK staff is much more that of being part of a peer-led community; innovation is encouraged and the taking of risks is, within limits, supported rather than criticised even when the outcomes are less than ideal.

This difference is not one that arises in a simple sense from the statutory/voluntary or local authority/independent distinction. Complex diverse organisations are less dominated by, or focused on, a single professional perspective. The local authority is concerned with a wide range of issues and problems and treats youth work as part of a mosaic of services. For the worker in Hillshire Council the trade-off is some loss of autonomy in exchange for an organisational commitment to a much wider view than can be taken by YWUK. In the local authority the youth worker has a potential line of communication with colleagues from a range of disciplines and with access to a much greater range of services. It might also be argued at the policy level that a strategic approach to young people's needs and interests is something that only a local authority can develop, given also that it is uniquely legitimated through local democratic processes and structures.

Parental–ethical

This label emerged as an appropriate characterisation of an organisation concerned to do the right thing but reluctant to trust the worker to make independent decisions about what courses of action to follow. In transactional analysis terms it would be seen as a 'controlling parent', and the emphasis on accountability through control or prescription by the organisation makes the notion of professionalism problematic. Some degree of autonomy is an important dimension of professionalism and it is therefore difficult to so characterise work in an organisation which functions in this way, even though such a culture might be found in many of the traditional professions. For example, in some types of hospital medical practice highly trained 'professional' staff are required to follow particular processes and procedures rather than exercising independent judgement.

It is not hard to find examples of settings where informal work with young people is conducted in such an atmosphere. Uniformed organisations with their quasi-military structures and symbols might be characterised in this way, emphasising quite specific schemes of work and a strong hierarchy. Similarly many organisations of the small voluntary club type operate effectively under the control of one strong individual, or at most a very small group. The Riverside Youth Club fits fairly neatly into this conceptual category, given its style and mode of organisation under the control of an acknowledged 'club leader'. There is nothing inherently problematic about such a climate. The dominant traditions in this particular group are respectful and caring towards young people, and encourage a progressive involvement by club members in decisions about the programme and activities. The critical tension in such a climate is likely to be between the dominant centre and potential alternative leadership. Alternative conceptions of purpose are effectively excluded unless control shifts from one dominant individual or group to a new centre of power. It is in this way that changes have taken place and the Riverside Youth Club has retained the interest of successive generations of young people over the years.

Regulatory–ethical

Here accountability is to an ideal or professional ethic. The worker's loyalty is at least as much to a wider community of practice, and to those they serve, as it is to the employer. Scope for autonomy is acknowledged and treated as an entitlement, albeit constrained by the organisation's concern with its reputation or public image. Workers cannot be permitted to exercise their discretion in ways that might appear to threaten that image. The central difficulty for the worker in this climate is to maintain commitment to the idealised notions of professional practice while avoiding transgression of the organisation's imposed norms.

YWUK and the Woodhouse Youth Project might both be mapped on to this quadrant although for slightly different reasons. The difference may be understood in terms of the source of moral authority; in YWUK the ethical boundaries are determined largely internally and are legitimated in part by the history and standing of the organisation. In the Woodhouse Project, by contrast, workers see the main source of authority lying outside the project itself, in the hands of funders. The mediation of this authority through the framework of an independent project creates a protective barrier and provides the project and its workers with the standing of autonomous professionals, but at the same time the constraint of 'funder acceptance' is rarely out of sight. Despite the ambiguities which are clearly present, such a climate might be seen as attractive by workers; it would perhaps be evidenced by a moderate turnover of staff, clear commitments to ethical practice in recruitment and selection, proactive training and staff development policies and innovative practice.

Professional–ethical

The combination of an organisation concerned at a corporate level to act ethically, and of individuals' independent accountability to a professional ethic might seem an ideal to strive towards. In practice, however, a number of potential difficulties may appear. The requirement for fully conscious decision-making by 'autonomous professionals' creates a level of demand on the individual worker that may be difficult to sustain. Primary reference to a community of practice rather than to organisational rules or simply custom and practice as the source of support in ethical decision-making might leave the individual experiencing isolation, doubt and uncertainty as a consequence of any dilemma with an ethical dimension.

In an important sense this conceptualisation is included only to complete the symmetry of the model. It seems to us unlikely that many youth workers will find themselves working in such a climate, although a lack of close scrutiny over practice and the isolation of individual workers sometimes creates the impression that one is working in an 'ethical' climate when the reality is more appropriately understood as an ineffective bureaucracy. As a work climate it might also lack the focus for debate and the resolution of conflict, although it could be claimed that this kind of debate is simply transferred from the immediate surroundings of the organisation to some professional forum where issues are explored, disputes resolved and transgressors sanctioned. It is better, in our view, for the nature and purpose of practice to be the focus of regular scrutiny and discussion by one's peers, in the context of practice rather than outside it.

There is probably little to be gained from any attempt to specify an 'ideal' climate. However, if pressed we would tend to concentrate on the stronger accountability axis and seek a position towards the idealised notion of accountability to a professional ethic rather than to organisational control. That is not, however, to suggest that other climates are unavoidably hostile. Climate as a metaphor allows us to suggest that professionalism may be quite a hardy organism, able to survive and even flourish in a range of situations. Extreme conditions, however, may require special approaches and may not offer long-term prospects for survival.

Conclusion

In this chapter we have seen that individuals, managers and organisations interact to facilitate or impede ethical practice in youth work, but that individual workers have the ability to interpret their own organisational context and act to integrate professional and organisational imperatives. Workers have a sense of agency, a belief that they can act to change the world that they are in and that they can make a difference. Individual conceptions of ethical practice that have been forged in professional training, discussions with fellow workers or through shared commitments to a particular value base will result in actions that may differ from those espoused by the organisation. For example, in terms of accountability there can be real disagreements, especially in organisations like Riverside, about how and to whom the service is responsive when disruptive young people are construed by some workers as needing support and by 'management' as spoiling the provision for the majority. What this chapter has sought to demonstrate is not that such disagreements are avoidable but that placing the exploration and resolution of debate at the heart of our work is essential. Ignoring the diversity of views that arise from the interactions in and between individuals and their organisations will not avoid disputes but simply 'displace them into discontent' (Fairley and Paterson 1995: 34). Being aware of the differing conceptions of professionalism, accountability and organisational context that we have explored is more likely to result in uncomfortable dilemmas and contradictions for individuals but, nevertheless, the struggle to resolve these will lead to growth and development and a more ethically based practice.

Bibliography

Airaksinen, T. (1994) 'Service and science in professional life' in R. Chadwick (ed.) *Ethics and the Professions*, Aldershot: Avebury.

Argyris, C. and Schon, D. (1974) *Theory in Practice: Increasing Professional Effectiveness*, San Francisco: Jossey Bass.

Banks, S. (1996) 'Youth work, informal education and professionalisation', *Youth and Policy* 54: 13–25.

Bloor, G. and Dawson, P. (1994) 'Understanding professional culture in organisational context', *Organisation Studies* 15(2): 275–95.

Bloxham, S. and Heathfield, M. (1995) 'Reflecting the theory/practice dichotomy in youth and community work training', *Youth and Policy* 50: 35–48.

Etzioni, A. (1969) *The Semi-Professions and their Organisation*, London: Collier Macmillan.

Fairley, J. and Paterson, L. (1995) 'Scottish education and the new managerialism', *Scottish Educational Review* 27(1): 13–36.

Friedson, E. (1986) *Professional Powers: A Study of the Institutionalisation of Formal Knowledge*, Chicago and London: University of Chicago Press.

Goffman, E. (1975) *Frame Analysis*, Harmondsworth: Penguin.

Henry, C. (1994) 'Professional behaviour and the organisation' in R. Chadwick (ed.) *Ethics and the Professions*, Aldershot: Avebury.

Holdsworth, D. (1994) 'Accountability: the obligation to lay oneself open to criticism' in R. Chadwick (ed.) *Ethics and the Professions*, Aldershot: Avebury.

Huxham, C. (ed.) (1996) *Creating Collaborative Advantage*, London: Sage.

Jackson, J. (1994) 'Common codes: divergent practices' in R. Chadwick (ed.) *Ethics and the Professions*, Aldershot: Avebury.

Milburn, T. (1994) 'Collaboration – it's the name of the game' *Concept* 4.1: 13–15.

Millar, G. (1995) 'Beyond managerialism', *Youth and Policy* 50: 49–58.

Mintzberg, H. (1979) *The Structuring of Organisations*, Englewood Cliffs, NJ: Prentice-Hall.

McCulloch, K. and Tett, L. (1995) 'Performance indicators as quality assurance: the Scottish Community Education PI Scheme', *Quality Assurance in Education* 4, 3: 17–26.

Scottish Office (1996) *The Public Inquiry into the Shootings at Dunblane Primary School on 13th March 1996 (Cullen Report)*, London: HMSO.

Smith, M. (1988) *Developing Youth Work*, Milton Keynes: Open University Press.

—— (1994) *Local Education*, Milton Keynes: Open University Press.

Victor, B. and Cullen, J. (1988) 'The organisational bases of ethical work climates', *Administrative Science Quarterly* 33: 101–25.

Weber, M. (1947) *The Theory of Social and Economic Organisation*, London: Oxford University Press.

Wilding, P. (1982) *Professional Power and Social Welfare*, London: Routledge and Kegan Paul.

4

RESOURCING YOUTH WORK

Dirty hands and tainted money

Tony Jeffs and Mark Smith

Introduction

Ever since modern youth work surfaced towards the end of the eighteenth century it has been strapped for cash. While uniformed and small local groups have managed with voluntary effort, larger clubs, settlements and centres have often struggled to raise sufficient money and to recruit volunteers. In this chapter we want to explore some of key issues that arise out of the need to raise money. Our inquiry is based around a review of literature within youth work and a series of interviews with managers and workers. We begin by reviewing some of the tensions between philanthropic, state and commercial funding, and then move on to examine questions around funding sources, canvassing and fund-raising methods.

Philanthropy and the state

Raising money, recruiting volunteers, gaining free or subsidised access to buildings, and living with the prospect of imminent closure have been the norm for most youth organisations and groups. Much of the money and assistance has come from young people themselves, their parents and other local people (Jeffs and Smith 1988). The role of the churches has been central – 'evangelicalism harnessed social conscience to liberal doctrine' (Prochaska 1988: 24) – and, in the past, there was a significant working-class involvement in non-conformist religious and other groups who were concerned with provision for children (Laqueur 1976) and young people (Smith 1988: 24–47). It is important to avoid falling into the trap of seeing philanthropy as something done by the rich to the poor.

Strong though the philanthropic impulse was, few youth workers questioned the desirability of state funding. Alternative sources were often capricious and fickle, as Robert Owen (founder of what was probably the first community education centre) and Hannah More (the pioneer of Sunday schooling) discovered (Hopkins 1947: 185–95). The latter advocated state rather than private funding: 'the charity of the rich should ever be subsidiary to the public provision in those numberless instances to which the most equal laws cannot apply' (More quoted in Collingwood and Collingwood 1990: 106).

Others such as William Lovett, who promoted Chartist clubs' education programmes in the 1840s, saw democratically controlled state funding as a means to avoid sectarian interference. They also wished to escape the clutches of those whom Thomas Carlyle dubbed the 'Aristocracy of the Moneybags' – rich philanthropists who frequently imposed stern conditions on the work. Yet it was not only rich benefactors who were a problem – local sponsors such as chapels and churches also had strong ideas about how the work should proceed.

A further argument for state involvement was picked up by some settlement and youth workers from social idealists such as T. H. Green. He viewed the state, in the right hands, as having the capacity to embrace superior moral characteristics to those which we might in normal circumstances encounter in the behaviour of the individual. In other words, the state could embody 'our higher self', more generous, caring and socially responsible than we might be in our daily lives. This philosophical position was indirectly transferred to a generation of public schoolboys and girls, with mixed degrees of success, emphasising the importance of 'team spirit' and the need for Christians to express their faith through service to others. To this intellectual foundation, educationalists such as Thomas Arnold added elements of the rough-and-ready ideological bedrock upon which boys' and girls' clubs, uniformed organisations and the settlement movement were constructed. Association, *esprit de corps* and sacrifice became ends and ideals. Predictably, there were tensions: for example, whether the provision of external funding encouraged a dependency culture which subverted the best efforts of youth workers to foster self-reliance. However, such trepidation never propagated a coherent or vocal opposition.

The rise of state funding

Once the principle of the state being the dominant provider of school and post-school education was accepted (along with its right to monitor the treatment of children in the home), state involvement in youth work became a foregone conclusion. From the late nineteenth century onwards youth and community workers were among the most shrill advocates of greater governmental interference in the lives of young people (Hendrick 1990, 1994; Jeffs 1979). Post-1918 there was barely a discernible ripple of concern regarding the potential dangers of unrestrained state interference in youth work. A state monopoly of youth work first occurred in Communist Russia, then Fascist Italy and finally, by 1933, in Nazi Germany. Some youth organisations initially saw positive benefits in this development (Stovin 1935). With the outbreak of war in 1939, advocacy of an all-embracing state youth service became distinctly muted. Instead a partnership of statutory and voluntary sectors became the desired model. Underpinning this concept was an implicit agreement whereby central and local government would fund youth provision to compensate for the inability of the voluntary sector to provide a comprehensive service. Governments recognised that for the partnership to succeed they would need to aid the voluntary sector via grants, the subsidisation of training and managerial support. Aside from any ideological considerations, self-interest contributed to this compromise. Any deterioration in the viability of the voluntary sector would have fuelled demands for an escalation of state expenditure.

Growth in state expenditure on youth work since 1945 has not followed a smoothly ascending trajectory. Up to the mid-1950s it declined sharply before rising slowly prior to a dramatic fillip following publication of the Albemarle Report (HMSO 1960). Since then the changing fortunes of the economy and pressures on ministers to do 'something about the youth problem' have created peaks and troughs (Jeffs and Smith 1988, 1994; Stenson and Factor 1994, 1995). While local authority youth service expenditure has dramatically declined since 1979 (Hawkins 1995; Maychell, Pathak and Cato 1996), new sources of funding have become available. New providers have entered the field in, for example, the arts, health promotion, environmental action, and as supplements to schooling and housing.

Initially, 'statutory' youth work, like schools, was financed by a mix of central government grants to Local Education Authorities and local taxation. However, the determination of the 1979–97 Conservative administration to curtail local government autonomy led to a partial dismantling of this arrangement. First, local authorities lost the capacity to set their own rate. Second, central government rechannelled resources from LEAs to unelected quasi-governmental bodies such as Development Corporations and Training and Enterprise Councils. These then invited both voluntary and statutory organisations to bid for funds. Third, partly to compensate for cutbacks in LEA provision but also to meet their own output targets, statutory bodies such as police and health authorities began bank-rolling of non-formal educational work with young people. Finally, the government-sponsored National Lottery has been used as an alternative means of funding 'good causes' including youth work.

Commercialisation and the 'new' youth work organisations

Coupled to these changes was a series of initiatives aimed at creating a political, economic and social climate which reinforced and reflected the values of the free market and which was hostile to collectivism. The government searched for ways of inserting free-market values and competition into the management and delivery of services. A contract culture was promoted whereby funding had to be fought for. Finance was increasingly time-limited and dependent upon 'evidence' that a programme could deliver measurable outputs (Read 1996). As ministers and officials endlessly reiterated, the public sector – practitioners and clients alike – must be taught that resources are scarce.

At a superficial level this ideological shift led to the appearance of meaningless mission statements and charters pinned to club walls, members becoming customers and youth workers dressing up in the garb of the entrepreneur. We have seen the introduction of a business vocabulary and managerialism that fails to address the distinctive purposes, conditions and tasks of public services (Stewart 1992). Such changes reflect a growing commercialisation of youth work. A process which is but a tiny component of the much more comprehensive political and ideological programme already mentioned.

Complex philosophical factors are involved in changing from a leader to a chief executive of a project – and to regard oneself as an entrepreneur instead of a worker; a director rather than team leader.

Such mutations are more than mere semantics, or a by-product of changing fashions. They reflect conscious or unconscious choices as to how individuals or organisations perceive their role, and where they locate themselves on an ideological continuum. Growing commercialisation has, for example, 'forced' projects to secure business sponsorship as a precondition for receiving other monies, put advertising on the back of membership cards, and required representatives of the so-called business community are appointed to management committees and governing bodies. These shifts have not occurred by accident. They flow, in part, from policy decisions made at the highest level. They are about ensuring that informal educators teach the values of the free market rather than collectivism; they encourage greed not sacrifice, consumption rather than restraint. The contract culture operates a 'hidden hand' which imposes a harsh discipline. It brooks little opposition and because all are judged by vague and imprecise criteria it does much to stifle criticism. One worker pointedly informed us that it 'has effectively silenced the voluntary sector. Line managers tell workers and they never argue about what they should prioritise' (youth worker, national voluntary agency).

Along with these movements we are also witnessing the emergence of 'new' youth work organisations (NYWOs) that mark a distinct break from previous forms. These agencies tend to have a strong business orientation and involve commercial interests more centrally in their management. Some, like Groundwork Trust, are funded by a range of public and private sources. Groundwork has developed various packages of work with schools and young people in partnership with organisations such as Esso and the National Grid. Significantly, Groundwork also runs services directed at small and medium-sized companies to 'gain business advantage through making the environment part of their long term planning and day to day management' (Groundwork 1996).

A further element that can often be found in the programmes of NYWOs is the attempt to encourage young people to see themselves as entrepreneurs and producers. Perhaps the most obvious examples of this arise in relation to projects around youth enterprise – but they also emerge in the arts and other fields. There are now a number of local agencies that specifically seek to develop the business acumen of young people and their ability to identify and exploit niche markets. Examples here include the provision of business units and support services, general education programmes around enterprise, money and support for business start-up (for example, the Prince's

Business Trust) and the formation of 'commercial arms' to produce and market goods and services such as furniture, videos, news items and environmental improvement.

Another feature of NYWOs tends to be an emphasis on developing, promoting and selling a 'distinctive' product or service. Organisations such as Citizen's Schools and Youth Action Programmes have designed specific packages that are marketed to local authorities and others in order to 'solve' a particular problem such as school non-attendance, the lack of homework support, or the usage of certain drugs. Some individual workers have also entered this arena, developing services and opportunities for young people that can be bought in by youth work providers. In many respects, this runs in line with movements in youth work provision in the USA where various not-for-profit agencies provide services.

It then becomes a small step into the provision of play and youth work services which are for profit. Examples of this are common within the field of 'leisure-time animation' in Italy and France (Lorenz 1994: 101), but there are also substantial initiatives in the UK, for example, in the commercial provision of adventure holidays and opportunities, and of play opportunities in shopping malls. This is likely to be an area of some growth as fast food chains such as McDonalds, leisure providers such as Warner Brothers and 'lifestyle' companies such as Virgin look for new markets that are close to their core businesses.

We believe that these changes regarding how youth work is oriented and funded require workers to confront some difficult ethical dilemmas. These occur in relation to three inter-linked issues:

- Should agencies actively canvass for funding?
- Are certain sources of funding ethically unacceptable?
- Are certain methods of collecting/obtaining funding ethically unacceptable?

We will now consider each of the above in turn, examining how workers have tried to make sense of practice in relation to ideas about what may make for the good.

Should agencies and workers actively canvass for funding?

Should youth organisations accept any external money at all? In the past workers have argued that to ask for money exposed them to accusations of self-interest and an absence of faith. In addition, it left them beholden to interests that ran counter to their mission. Typical of these were Georg Müller in England and William Quarrier in Scotland, who were both involved in developing orphanages and young people's communities, and each of whom saw their work as revealing the will of God. They postulated that so long as they followed His direction all would be well:

> The work was the Lord's and William Quarrier only his agent. God would provide. Accordingly there never was an appeal for money, no bazaars to raise funds, no envelope collection. It was an enterprise in faith from the beginning.
>
> (Ross 1971: 13)

Müller likewise never pleaded for or solicited funds (Pierson 1902). Thomas Barnardo had little patience for such individuals describing them as a 'race of philanthropists and Evangelists who live on faith and postage stamps' (quoted in Wagner 1979: 198). Today, when the chase for funding often seems all-consuming, it might be worth briefly reflecting on their position.

Many workers are being forced to devote more and more time to fund-raising at the expense of face-to-face work. Of course some prefer attending fund-raising events, writing letters and mixing with 'movers and shakers' to the company of young people and the local community. Others recognise what is happening and resent it, yet a sense of duty drives them on. As a drugs project worker admitted when interviewed, five years ago she spent a few weeks a year on public relations and fund-raising, now it occupies the equivalent of two months and is still expanding. She knew a line would have to be drawn but was not sure when. She acknowledged the work with clients was being devalued and 'pushed aside'. However, she was under intense pressure to keep the project going. The young people and part-time workers saw it as important and would be loathe to see it close. However, was it right, she wondered, to put so much effort into 'raising my own salary'?

The question here is less whether active canvassing is wrong and more about the extent. How then do workers make judgements in this area? Do they confine themselves to seeking out core or essential funding, or do they simply view fund-raising as a fact of life? One 'solution' favoured by Breen (1993: 158) is to look to young people. He abandoned the centre which consumed all his time and energy to maintain and left him too exhausted to 'concentrate on relationships'. Rather than worry about buildings and resources, he insisted that if the young people you work with want money for a project or somewhere to meet, they must secure these for themselves, perhaps with help from workers. For Breen the role of the worker is not dispenser of resources, which inevitably creates a 'provider–client' relationship leading to 'patronising attitudes' (ibid.: 50) but to be an educator, friend and ally. This approach, of course, still leaves important ethical questions for the group. Who should they accept money from, what strings should be attached, how much effort should they put into the activity?

Robert Woods, the pioneer American settlement and club worker, viewed dependency on philanthropy as an ever-present threat encouraging workers to avoid the difficult task of engaging with the community and involving local people. Instead, it motivated them to devote their attention to the wealthy who could endow the club with money and to overlook the poor who could only offer their time and talents. Therefore to

> canvass for money would be as much against our principles as a canvass for information, and I think it would be better to get acquainted gradually with local citizens and to educate them by object lessons as to their duty.
>
> (Woods 1929: 68)

Few workers would be willing to risk adopting the sort of position Quarrier, Breen and Woods advocate. The interviewee who informed us he did not bother looking for '£500 from Mr and Mrs Bloggs, I am looking for big money and want to get in with the big players' would, we suspect, have little sympathy with it. Yet many reading this could compile a list of projects where dangerous confusion has arisen regarding ends and means. The result can be that staff invest disproportionate energy and resources in sustaining the project, the building or their own salaries at the expense of the needs of the clientele. They may well exploit young people and other workers in doing so, as the following extract from an interview shows:

> [The management] wanted the funding but they didn't want me. They never really bothered with me or helped or supported me in any serious way. I was just left to see out

my time, they had no intention of following up or continuing any of the work I started. It was a disgrace.

Refusing to solicit for funding is one way to avoid this temptation and dilemma. It will not of course eliminate such temptation
but it can encourage a much clearer focus of the role and purpose
for the work.

Are certain sources of funding ethically unacceptable?

Many workers have grappled with questions such as 'how can we
fund our work without subverting the values which underpinned
it?' A nun working with homeless young people recounted such a
tension. She saw the work as 'helping people to value themselves,
to feel at peace with who they are, to recognise their worth and
gifts and creating opportunities for them to contribute'. She
continued:

> I resist talking of the work as a 'project' and I try to avoid
> chasing money as I feel it is so easy to get caught in that
> trap and in the latest trends. I get people telling me about
> the sources of money and they seem surprised when I seem
> not to be interested...I just wonder if we could just become
> like everyone else in the sense of moving into 'in' areas of
> work, where the money is. This shouldn't be what we are
> about. I think we must be distinctive in the sense we are
> part of the wider church, of the transcendent, part of
> working for something bigger, standing for a set of values
> and principles, centred on the Gospel and not on the
> market or state.

She also described the disbelief bordering on outrage when she
suggested to colleagues and supporters they should no longer be a
registered charity. She argued that such a status demeaned and stig-
matised those they worked with and created in the minds of the
workers a false perception of their role.

Even where organisations have refused to canvas or chase
funding, they are still left with the question of what money
to accept and to refuse. In our review, three key themes
appeared:

- does taking money from certain sources seriously undermine the moral authority of the workers?
- does the form funding takes stigmatise young people?
- are the 'strings' attached acceptable?

Sources of funding and the moral authority of workers

In 1891, after working at Hull House for a number of years with a group of young women, Jane Addams perceived the need for a Girls' Club linked to the settlement but with its own building. After sharing this with colleagues and supporters a trustee informed Addams that a friend had offered to donate the $20,000 required to open a clubhouse. Subsequently she learnt the prospective donor was a man notorious for underpaying the young women in his establishment and about whom 'even darker stories' were circulating. Following heated exchanges amongst trustees, staff and members the donation was dubbed 'tainted money' and returned. Her position was that:

> social changes can only be inaugurated by those who feel the unrighteousness of contemporary conditions, and the expression of their scruples may be one opportunity for pushing forward moral tests into that dubious area wherein wealth is accumulated.
>
> (Addams 1930: 139)

Addams was not alone in this. A worker at one New York settlement insisted on his right to speak out against the use of tainted money even where trustees and colleagues opted for acceptance. So determined was he to retain his autonomy on this matter that a letter of resignation was lodged with the trustees which could be executed at any time. Similarly Lilian Wald, founder of the Henry Street Settlement in New York, who was a pacifist, objected in 1916 to the trustees investing in Bethlehem Steel which was profiting from war orders.

According to Carson, the majority of American settlement and club workers during this period did not share the position of Wald and Addams. Not only did they refrain from questioning the origins of a donation but they also tempered campaigns against sweated labour, slum landlords and political corruption to avoid offending 'prosperous and often "conservative" uptown patrons' (Carson 1990: 53). The latter group came to dominate and the issue of 'tainted money', which attracted so much attention within the settlement and club movement in America around the turn of the century, largely faded from view.

Certain religious groups have, however, consistently avoided taking money from specific sources. As a worker related, 'because it is a Methodist church...you couldn't apply to somewhere like a brewery, or somewhere to do with tobacco. Also you can't apply to certain lotteries.' Not only agencies controlled by certain religious bodies have to negotiate this issue. We were told of an ecumenical youth housing project which withdrew a National Lottery bid, despite a serious risk it would fold, because the long-standing representative of the Baptist Church on the steering group said she would resign if they proceeded. The money was raised from elsewhere, the majority holding that her departure would erode the ecumenical heart of the project. Others, though, construct somewhat tenuous ways of getting around their principles. One Methodist centre, for example, agreed: 'you can't apply for money to do things to the building...but you can for a project that directly tackles poverty'.

Some are unequivocal regarding their position. A representative of the Girls' Brigade explained why they would not accept Lottery funds:

> We exist to offer girls a Christian viewpoint on life and it would be completely inconsistent to teach them to value and serve other people while the organisation itself accepted funding from a source where people can only gain by the loss of others.
>
> (quoted by Tondeur 1996)

The debate regarding whether or not National Lottery funding is acceptable has predominately been shaped by competing religious positions around gambling (Tondeur 1996; see also Perkins 1933). Yet the debate has implications for all workers, and serves as a contemporary example of the 'tainted money' predicament. It requires workers to consider how acceptance might undermine their moral authority.

Does receipt of lottery funding, for example, help to legitimise participation in this, and other, forms of gambling? The sale of lottery cards to under-sixteens is illegal. Despite this, one survey showed 21 per cent of 14-year-old boys purchased tickets during the week studied and 62 per cent of retailers flouted the law (*Young People*

Now 1997: 13). For many youth workers and teachers to point a disapproving finger at such shopkeepers smacks of hypocrisy. Their eagerness to grab a share of the profits from such sales, plus the unashamed way many boast of their 'success' in securing such spoils, surely makes it impossible for them to continue to express disapproval of gambling amongst the young. Further, the lottery has blatantly sought respectability by aligning itself with good causes to put 'clear blue water' between itself and what it hopes will become classified as less reputable forms of gambling. It has targeted youth organisations to both tempt future customers and because 'young people' and youthful activities can bestow a clean, healthy image.

National Lottery funding is not of itself 'tainted money'. Those who enjoy a flutter at the racecourse or see a poker school as a place where skills are exercised and social networks forged, may with justification sneer at the intellectual vacuum at the heart of the proceedings but can scarcely judge the resulting handouts as tainted. However, those who seek to discourage gambling in the young will find it difficult to do otherwise. Sadly, the growing dependency of youth organisations upon National Lottery suborns has not stimulated a serious discussion concerning either the place of gambling within youth work or the case for or against retaining prohibitions which prevent young people from gambling.

At specific times some groups have sought to disassociate themselves from particular firms. For a period Barclays Bank was boycotted by student unions and a number of community projects for its links with South Africa. More recently, Nestlé has been similarly treated because of its policies of marketing baby milk products in developing countries. However, in the sometimes murky world of charity fund-raising the spectre of a company with such public relations difficulties has acted as a spur to an approach by an agency. Indeed we know of at least two national organisations providing services for young people who sell themselves to such companies with the message, 'fund us and it will help you gain a healthier profile'. Companies such as BP, which from time to time have hit problems with environmental groups, have been quick to put money into environmental projects aimed at young people and to advertise this with the endorsement, for example, of Youth Clubs UK (BP 1997).

Without exception those interviewed said they would decline a donation from a cigarette company. Cynics might point out that, unlike the National Lottery, major environmental polluters and

exploiters of Third World child labour such as the leading manufacturers of sporting goods, cigarette manufacturers have never
sponsored youth work on any scale, so disapproval requires no
sacrifice.

Does stigmatisation result?

In raising money there is a tendency to paint an exaggerated image
of young people as both victims, needing help, and a threat to
society, needing to be managed. Several workers voiced their
concern about the apparent way that young people have to be
presented in order to gain funding. Over the years there has been a
fairly consistent appeal to moral panics as a way of selling youth
work (Jeffs and Smith 1988: 14–40). As a local authority youth
work adviser commented: 'If you want money it is now a matter of
promising to do something about crime or graffiti to get your hands
on it'.

Whether it is youth crime, sexual health, drug addiction or
school under-achievement, fears about these can be appealed to and
youth work offered as part of a solution. The result has been a
series of funding initiatives that target particular behaviours and
groups. To access such money agencies then have to 'fit' those they
work with, or seek to work with, into sets of often stereotypical and
sometimes demeaning categories. If they gain funding, workers then
have to justify what they have done in relation to the same problematic categories. The result can be either a subversion of the work –
typically at the moment involving a pandering to the new authoritarianism (Jeffs and Smith 1994) or problems in reporting. The
latter can entail straightforward lying or presenting work in alternative ways (which may not be to the satisfaction of the funder).
As one worker put it:

> I realize that some colouring of the facts might be neces-
> sary to get money for this community, but it is getting
> ridiculous. To get...[some funding]...I now have a choice.
> Change the way I work or lie.

A further fear is that by participating in such categorisation,
youth work organisations confirm a picture of young people as
thugs, victims or users. Their work is presented to funders as
helping to 'solve' a problem with young people. Simultaneously, this
strengthens a popular prejudice and undermines practice that may

have strengthened those young people's sense of worth and possibility.

Conditions and strings

Issues around the strings attached to funding take many forms and can relate to the way in which young people are presented (see above), to the sorts of activities that may be involved, and to practical issues around when and how money may be spent. However, there have been persistent worries around conditions concerning the direction youth work takes.

Considerable discussion has occurred regarding the extent to which a worker could legitimately seek to change the lifestyle or beliefs of young people. Controversy has centred on matters of faith and patriotism. Some organisations have been open regarding their determination to convert. As a founder of the YWCA explained, a central role was to release girls 'enchained by Judaism, Popery, and heathenism' (quoted in Moor 1910: 244). Yet flagrant attempts to train and convert are difficult to square with the role of the youth worker as educator. For as Peters argues, the role of the educator is to initiate young people 'into skill, attitudes and knowledge which are necessary for them to participate intelligently as citizens of a democratic state' not to act 'as a missionary for any church or as a recruiting officer for any political party' (1966: 203).

Loss of empire and professionalisation of the armed forces has virtually eradicated pressure on youth workers to prepare young people for military service, while the declining influence of religious bodies in public life has generally liberated those not directly employed by them from the role of missionary. Indeed the pendulum has swung in the opposite direction: those who over energetically seek to convert young people risk dismissal from most secular agencies.

Nowadays, pressure to serve as a missionary or recruiting sergeant has been supplanted by coercion to perform as a huckster for particular brands and products. Multinational companies and local rivals increasingly target educational agencies to ensure they produce not the 'perfect' worker but compliant 'dumb-downed' consumers. Youth workers are, like other educators, being bribed to create marketing opportunities for firms anxious to capture consumers while they are of an 'impressionable age'. In return for sponsorship, they are being 'persuaded' to endorse products by putting up advertisements in centres, adding company logos to membership cards, reports, leaflets and notepaper, and promoting marketing ploys such as discount cards. An example is the decision of the Scout Association to allow firms to buy space on merit badges linked to their area of interest for between £5,000 and £50,000. For example, for achievement in athletics the symbol of the runner rests on the name of a running shoe manufacturer. It is a system which not only enables corporations to target advertising, but equally the payment secures them the tacit endorsement of a youth organisation with a reputation for probity and generates '700,000 trustworthy, walking advertisements' (Tran 1990: 6).

In the nineteenth century a compliant government encouraged religious organisations to corrupt the educational process by restricting the access of young people to open dialogue, honest debate and untainted knowledge. Today equally supine politicians encourage business organisations to do the same. Whereas their predecessors usually had the excuse that they sincerely believed they were saving the souls of the young, nowadays greed provides the motive for the donors and a craven desire to cut public spending serves as the political justification.

To this has been added a further issue. Some agencies are selling the young people they work with as marketing opportunities. In the United States, in return for cash, thousands of schools have installed televisions tuned to a predetermined station in classrooms, corridors and canteens. These pump out advertisements and promotional material aimed at young people who cannot choose an alternative programme or switch off the set and, because attendance is compulsory, they have no choice but to watch it (Apple 1993). In the UK, firms such as Tesco have effectively used schools and other educational agencies to bring moral pressure on children and their parents to shop in their stores – much to the profit of the store (Hoggart 1995: 32).

Sponsorship also leads to young people and youth workers being used as billboards. Payments often require them to wear T-shirts and hats advertising particular products or the name of their sponsors. Cohen reports the example of a reading enrichment programme sponsored by News International where children are kitted out in T-shirts carrying the names and logos of Rupert Murdoch's papers. By a 'total coincidence' the *Sun* publicised the support given the scheme by the prime minister. However, as Cohen (1997: 8) points out, those children who read about it in the *Sun* would have found on the page opposite a gigantic picture of a topless Melinda Messenger, with artificially enlarged breasts. 'Thigh love Mel!' read the headline on a report that a man had a picture of the model tattooed on his thigh. On the front page was a picture of Diana, Princess of Wales, on a jet-ski with Dodi al-Fayed headlined 'Di's legover'.

Arguing that we should not unduly worry because young people are too sophisticated to be taken in ignores the research of the advertisers which tells them who to target, and independent investigation which confirms not only are young people susceptible to advertising but that it is the least well-educated who are the most vulnerable (Balding *et al.* 1996).

Are certain methods of gaining funding ethically unacceptable?

Many youth organisations pay considerable attention to the 'how' of raising income. At the centre of this concern can be a desire to ensure that the methods employed avoid subverting the moral values and teachings of the organisation. There is also the hope that young people will learn socially useful lessons from involvement in the process of collection. As might be expected, the importance of consistency is stressed for, as Barrow points out, if an educator or leader says you should do this then they are committing themselves to the view that they and those they teach 'ought also to do this in the same circumstances' (1975: 52). As Colquhoun explains, the Scout Law sets the highest possible standards for boys to aspire to. Therefore, all connected to the organisation must set themselves a 'higher standard in regard to methods of raising money than others do' (1954: 68). Indeed the rules of the Scout Movement state 'money should be earned and not solicited' (ibid.: 69). Henriques was similarly determined that within the Boys' Club Movement all those involved should contribute something for:

> anything that savours of charity in the minds of the boys is obnoxious and distasteful to the highest degree...all boys must contribute, 'pauperization in a boys' club is loathsome'.
>
> (Henriques 1933: 211)

Avoidance of begging reflects a desire not to exploit the young people. Traditionally, this has been interpreted as not using their labour to sustain an organisation which has been established to serve them. This, for example, was the basis of the objections voiced within the Boys' Brigade to the launching in 1921 of B-B Week when members were sent out to raise money. Although these criticisms were set aside, it still remains an area of contention to this day within some organisations. For it is generally assumed that although young people should make some financial contribution in order to give them a stake and avoid 'pauperization', this should be more than balanced by a contribution from elsewhere.

The examples of sponsorship discussed not only exploit young people but also corrupt the educational process. As a worker pointed out, all too often it means increasingly 'projects have to be constructed around what will attract sponsorship rather than what we as workers choose to believe is needed'. This also leads to the expressed needs of the young people being relegated to the margins. Another said: 'Unless we find an alternative...then our young people will be locked into a slavery of intellect and a servility of attitude'.

A further set of questions arises around the way in which many youth organisations have enthusiastically embraced business interests and partners. In the NYWOs there tends to be less of a tension between their expressed aims and their mode of operation. If they see themselves as businesses, then it is fairly easy and consistent to view young people as customers. Within those local authorities and agencies that have gone the 'charter' route there has been a significant pressure from the centre to promote 'customer care' and 'customer satisfaction'. The problem for youth work is that it involves a fundamental misreading of both the educational process and the ultimate aims of the work. To view young people as consumers is to see them essentially as objects to be acted upon; services are, like pizzas, 'delivered' to them. If we are to approach the work in a proper educational spirit, then rather than being consumers, young people need to be engaged with as active participants, creators of their own meanings and possibilities.

Conclusion

An inevitable consequence of the voluntary nature of the relationship between young people and youth workers is that the latter, perhaps more than most educators, rely on their moral authority to secure a constituency. Securing and retaining such authority, often in trying circumstances, creates an ever present tension within the work, for without resorting to subterfuge they must seek to become the kind of people that the young 'can trust, both intellectually and with regard to their character...steady, completely reliable and consistent' (Warnock 1993: 23). Consequently, they need to pay careful attention to their reputation. How an organisation raises its income tells us a great deal about under-pinning values and ethics. Since the young people affiliated to an organisation are likely to be aware of the source of funding and how it was raised – indeed they often help procure it – workers can never totally sidestep the questions raised here regarding whether agencies should actively canvass for funding and whether certain sources and particular methods of collection and obtaining funding are ethically unacceptable?

Present funding arrangements disadvantage those who seek to operate according to ethical considerations. Part of the problem is that many funders have not considered these kinds of ethical questions. As one agency manager put it:

> The thing which was important is that these people hadn't thought about the issues until we went and asked them about funding. The ethical dimension had simply been absent.

Many youth work agencies are equally guilty of the same crime.

Just how workers and agencies can be encouraged to consider ethical questions is open to considerable debate. Some may want to go the route of writing a policy statement (in much the same way that equal opportunities statements have appeared). However, adoption of policy statements can mean little unless the questions approached are wrestled with. There is certainly a case for looking at training and such professional forums that exist within the work. Relatively little attention is given to explorations of what might make for the good in practice. The current technical focus on issue-based work and upon competencies tends towards the 'correct' rather than what is 'right' (see Jeffs and Smith 1990: 17–18, 124–43). This disposition to 'rule-following' and safety first tends to sideline active consideration of what might be good – and as such is anti-educational. Engaging with ethical questions around funding, and involving people within that conversation, is a central task for workers and agencies, and without which claims to moral authority wither away.

Acknowledgements

We would like to acknowledge our gratitude to those who allowed themselves to be interviewed and record our thanks to those who helped us do the interviewing: Phil Watson, Sarah Hackett and Huw Blacker.

Bibliography

Addams, J. (1930) *Twenty Years at Hull House*, New York: Macmillan.

Apple, M. (1993) *Official Knowledge: Democratic Education in a Conservative Age*, New York: Routledge.

Balding, J., Regis, D., Wise, A., Bish, D. and Muirden, J. (1996) *Bully Off: Young people that fear going to school*, Exeter: Schools Health Education Unit, University of Exeter.

Barrow, R. (1975) *Moral Philosophy for Education*, London: Unwin.

BP (1997) 'Thanks to BP, teenagers in Newburgh attend a regular board meeting', advertisement, *New Statesman*, 7 November: 60.

Breen, M. (1993) *Outside In: Reaching Unreached Young People Today*, London: Scripture Union.

Carson, M. (1990) *Settlement Folk: Social Thought and the American Settlement Movement 1885–1930*, Chicago: University of Chicago Press.

Cohen, N. (1997) 'Murdoch ate my banter' *Observer*, 31 August: 8.

Collingwood, J. and Collingwood, M. (1990) *Hannah More*, Oxford: Lion Publishers.

Colquhoun, J. F. (1954) *Running a Scout Troop*, London: Boy Scout Association.

Groundwork Trust (1996) *Partnerships with Business* http://www.groundwork.org.uk.

Hawkins, P. (1995) *Formula Funding and Financial Delegation in Youth Services and Adult Education*, Leicester: Youth Work Press.

Hendrick, H. (1990) *Images of Youth: Age, Class and the Male Youth Problem 1880–1920*, Oxford: Clarendon Press.

—— (1994) *Child Welfare: England 1872–1989*, London: Routledge.

Henriques, B. (1933) *Club Leadership*, London: Oxford University Press.

HMSO (1960) *The Youth Service in England and Wales* (The Albemarle Report), London: HMSO.

Hoggart, R. (1995) *The Way We Live Now*, London: Chatto and Windus.

Hopkins, M. A. (1947) *Hannah More and her Circle*, New York: Longmans, Green.

Jeffs, A. J. (1979) *Young People and the Youth Service*, London: RKP.

Jeffs, T. and Smith, M. (1988) 'The political economy of youth work' in T. Jeffs and M. Smith (eds) *Welfare and Youth Work Practice*, London: Macmillan.

—— (eds) (1990) *Using Informal Education: An Alternative to Casework,*

Teaching and Control?, Buckingham: Open University Press.

—— (1994) 'Young People, Youth Work and a New Authoritarianism' *Youth and Policy* 46: 17–32.

Kingman, J. M. and Sidman, E. (1935) *A Manual of Settlement Boys' Work*, Boston: National Federation of Settlements.

Korten, D. C. (1995) *When Corporations Rule the World*, West Hartford CT: Kumarian Press.

Laqueur, T. W. (1976) *Religion and Respectability: Sunday Schools and Working Class Culture*, New Haven: Yale University Press.

Lorenz, W. (1994) *Social Work in a Changing Europe*, London: Routledge.

Maychell, K., Pathak, S. and Cato, V. (1996) *Providing for Young People: Local Authority Youth Services in the 1990s*, Slough: NFER.

Moor, L. M. (1910) *Girls of Yesterday and Today: The Romance of the YWCA*, London: Partridge.

Perkins, E. B. (1933) *Gambling and Youth*, London: National Sunday School Union.

Peters, R. S. (1966) *Ethics and Education*, London: Unwin.

Pierson, A. T. (1902) *George Müller of Bristol*, London: Pickering and Inglis.

Prochaska, F. (1988) *The Voluntary Impulse: Philanthropy in Modern Britain,* London: Faber and Faber.

Read, P. (1996) 'A quest for funding', *Young People Now* 89: 24–5.

Ross, J. (1971) *The Power I Pledge: A study of the life of William Quarrier*, Bridge of Weir: Quarrier's Homes.

Smith, M. (1988) *Developing Youth Work: Informal Education, Mutual Aid and Popular Practice*, Milton Keynes: Open University Press.

Stenson, K. and Factor, F. (1994) 'Youth work, risk and crime prevention' *Youth and Policy* 46: 1–15.

—— (1995) 'Governing youth: new directions for the youth service' in J. Baldock and M. May (eds) *Social Policy Review* 7, Canterbury: Social Policy Association.

Stewart, J. (1992) 'Guidelines for public service management: lessons not to be learnt from the private sector', in P. Carter, T. Jeffs and M. K. Smith (eds) *Changing Social Work and Welfare*, Buckingham: Open University Press.

Stovin, H. (1935) *Totem: The Exploitation of Youth*, London: Methuen.

Tondeur, K. (1996) *What Price the Lottery?*, Crowborough: Monarch Publications.

Tran, M. (1990) 'Keep Boy Scouts Pure' *Guardian* 31 December.

Wagner, G. (1979) *Barnardo*, London: Weindenfeld and Nicolson.

Warnock, M. (1993) 'Good Teaching' in R. Barrow and P. White (eds) *Beyond Liberal Education: Essays in Honour of Paul H. Hirst*, London: Routledge.

Woods, E. H. (1929) *Robert A Woods: A Biography*, Cambridge, Mass: Riverside Press.

Young People Now (1997) 'It could be your retailer' *Young People Now* 97: 13.

Part II

ETHICAL ISSUES IN PRACTICE

5

THE YOUTH WORKER AS GUIDE, PHILOSOPHER AND FRIEND

The realities of participation and empowerment

Kerry Young

Introduction

This chapter explores youth work's contribution to young people's moral deliberations and learning. In doing so, it examines the nature of the relationships and circumstances which can best support young people to reflect on their beliefs and interrogate the principles of their own moral judgements. Young people's participation is therefore understood in terms of their informed consent to engage in the process of moral philosophising necessarily involved. As a consequence, empowerment is not only the result of young people's increasing critical engagement and their growth towards autonomy; but also their developing ability to overcome both the external situations and internal forces which act to constrain their lives, their actions and their imaginations.

Purpose

Youth work is and always has been concerned with the development of young people's values. From its beginning, commitments to 'the improvement of the spiritual and mental condition of young men' (YMCA 1844 Statement of Purpose, in YMCA 1987: 4), the development of 'the whole personality of individual boys and girls' (HMSO 1940: para. 2) and the desire for young people to 'better equip themselves to live the life of mature, creative and responsible members of a free society' (Maud 1951: 3), all expressed aspirations which were centrally concerned not with the activities in which young people participated but with the values they held and the 'kind of people' they were to become. Indeed, the early voluntary youth organisations were often explicit about the desire to inculcate particular values and virtues in young people. Often framed in specifically religious or militaristic terms, these frequently included qualities such as obedience, discipline, punctuality and public service – and in some instances, a commitment to God, Queen and country (Davies and Gibson 1967; Eggleston 1976; Booton 1985; Smith 1988). Later, the Youth Advisory Council (1945: 10) proposed that 'whatever the activity and whatever the precise motif, the lessons to be learned are the same, co-operation, tolerance, free decision and joint responsibility.' In 1960, the Albemarle Report declared that the youth service was responsible for helping young people develop 'a sense of fellowship', 'the capacity to make sound judgements', and 'mutual respect and tolerance' (HMSO 1960: 37).

In a sense therefore, the desired outcomes of youth work have always been clearly stated and this is no less true in the 1990s than it ever was. Indeed, since its inception youth work has been continually refashioned to address contemporary concerns. More recently, attempts to attract changing sources of funding have usually been accompanied by promises to elicit from young people whatever behaviour was required by the particular funding body. As a result, youth work has been remodelled to fit the relevant criteria whether this concerned programmes for the unemployed, intermediate treatment, life skills training, health promotion, sex and drugs education, crime prevention, improving school attendance, combating alienation or social exclusion.

Whilst this has enabled the maintenance and development of certain aspects of provision for young people, the overall effect has been to obscure the fundamental purpose of youth work and confuse the public – including young people and sometimes the youth service itself. For in the process, not only has youth work been continually redefined, but young people have been constantly recast into different marginalised groups – street gangs in the 1960s; unemployed in the 1970s; at risk in the 1980s; and now in the 1990s, it seems, they swell the ranks of the disadvantaged. All of this is, of course, partly true insofar as some young people are at risk, unemployed, alienated, disadvantaged, and so on. But is the service's recurring metamorphosis a manifestation of its eagerness to meet the challenge of change or is it simply an indication that it has lost its way?

Youth work focuses its attention at a particular period in young people's lives. It is a period characterised by physiological and psychological changes as well as external (and often contradictory) pressures, expectations and demands from peers, adults and society at large. The extent to which it is necessarily a period of rebellion or alternatively adjustment is a matter of conjecture. What is clear however is that, in this society at least, adolescence brings with it a 'status ambiguity' (Coleman 1992: 9) and a sense of being in 'transition'. This is not to suggest that this period of transition is a shared experience. Indeed, the 'transition to responsible adulthood' (NYA 1997) is often experienced very differently depending on each young person's particular circumstances, as well as structural factors such as race, class, gender and sexuality.

Notwithstanding, the youth service has traditionally understood this period in young people's lives as 'a time for exploring the boundaries of freedom', of 'asking oneself questions about personal identity' and examining 'how one sees oneself and is seen by others' (Leighton 1972: 54). It is understood as a time of 'increased emotional awareness and spiritual or idealistic development' (Brew 1957: 18) and a time for asking the questions 'what sort of person am I?' and 'what sort of person am I going to be?' (Davies and Gibson 1967: 51). The young person is perceived as poised:

> to achieve a set of values drawn from ethical concepts and a growing moral conscience which makes him [sic] out as different to others in the way he views the social scene and relates to it.
>
> (Leighton 1972: 54)

In deliberately engaging with young people at this point in their lives youth workers are inevitably involved in discussions about what 'is' and what 'ought to be' – not simply from a prudential point of view but from a moral one.

This is neither accidental nor incidental. Indeed, it is in the nature of youth work to ask questions about what is right or wrong, good or bad, desirable or undesirable, acceptable or intolerable in individuals and in society. And it was for this reason, no doubt, that the Milson Fairbairn Report commented:

we find ourselves unable to answer the question 'what kind of Youth Service do we want?' until we have answered a previous question 'what kind of society do we want?'.

(HMSO 1969: 59)

The process of discussing, understanding and mediating values therefore underpins the very concept of youth work. It constitutes what Barrow calls a 'logical connection' (1981: 44) in the sense that the connection between youth work and values cannot be broken without distorting the nature of one or the other of the elements. This is very different from an understanding of youth work which locates 'values' in relation to access – for example:

Youth Work offers its services to young people regardless of their ethnicity, gender, social class, ability, religious affiliation or sexual orientation.

(Brown and Draper 1997: 25)

or indeed method:

Youth Work is informed by a set of beliefs which include a commitment to equal opportunity, and to young people as partners in learning and decision making.

(ibid.: 25)

For at the heart of youth work lies Socrates' question 'how should one live?' – which is both singular and plural in the sense that it asks 'how should I live?' as well as 'how should anyone live?' (Williams 1993: 20). These are questions about the kind of people we are and the kind of lives we believe we *ought* to lead. They are questions about our values – 'an enduring belief that a specific mode of conduct or end state of existence is personally or socially preferable to an opposite or converse mode of conduct or end state of existence' (Rokeach 1973: 5). And whilst all values are not moral values, they are all nonetheless based, fundamentally, on some conception of what is good and what is right. The issue of values in youth work is therefore not a question of access or method but rather the issue of young people's moral education – their deliberation about the good and the right, for individuals and society.

This focus on values is not new, since society has long been concerned with young people's sense of right and wrong, good and bad; and importantly their conformity to certain conventional standards of moral conduct. Notwithstanding, the emergence of the 'values education' movement (Robb 1996a, 1996b; Guide Association 1996; NCVYS 1997), the recent initiative to establish a 'code of ethics' for youth and community work (Ymlaen 1997: 8), the continued development of practice to challenge inequality, discrimination and oppression (Jeffs and Smith 1990; Thompson 1993; Dalrymple and Burke 1995) and widespread interest in 'emotional intelligence' (Goleman 1996) have all added new impetus to otherwise tired debates about values and equal opportunities in youth work. However, values-specific work with young people can be approached from different starting points. For example:

1   Some approaches presuppose the existence of a relatively fixed structure of values, virtues and dispositions into which young people are to be initiated – an approach frequently reflected in the often specifically religious initiatives of the early youth work organisations (Booton 1985; Smith 1988). Indeed, so prevalent was this approach that the Albemarle Committee felt it necessary to comment:

    The Youth Service should not seek to offer something packaged – 'a way of life', a 'set of values', 'a code of conduct' as though these were things which came ready-made, upon the asking, without being tested in living experience...If they feel the need young people must have the liberty to question cherished ideas, attitudes and standards and if necessary to reject them.
                                                    (HMSO 1960: 141)

2   'Values clarification' (popular in US schools in the 1960s and 1970s) adopts a systematic approach to helping young people become aware of their beliefs and behaviour in different practical situations. This approach, which built on the work of Louis Raths (1966), uses questionnaires and structured exercises to help young people think about how they come to hold certain values and beliefs and how these affect their behaviour.

3   More recently the National Forum for Values in Education and the Community (1996) sought to gain consensus for a particular set of values to be promoted in schools. Whilst the proposed values statements were intended only as a framework, there was a clear intention that the work of schools was

expected to contribute to changing young people's behaviour in particular prescribed ways.

4   Developments in values education seek to encourage young people to:

make explicit those values underlying their own attitudes; to assess the effectiveness of these values for their and others' long-term well-being and to reflect on and acquire other values which are more effective for their short-term and long-term well-being.

(Gordon Cook Foundation, quoted in Lewes 1996: 16)

With the exception of the first position (which could be termed moral training) the other approaches could be seen to be in the realm of moral education in the sense that they focus on the development of the 'cognitive equipment needed for autonomous moral judgement...not just or mostly [as] a matter of moral reasoning, but a growth in our concern for what we are in our relationships with each other' (Kleinig 1982: 252).

What has not been addressed however, is the question of context. That is, in what kind of context do young people learn to deliberate and mediate values, not in a mechanistic sense, but in terms of the circumstances which best support their learning. According to Kleinig (1982: 253) moral education is:

a matter of becoming a certain kind of person – of coming to care in certain kinds of ways and this is not directly achievable by means of syllabi and classroom techniques of the familiar kind. As much as anything, the development of virtue is a function of the relationships within which people move, and which provide a context for whatever moral reflection they engage in.

Relationships

Youth work has for many years affirmed the importance of the youth worker–young person relationship. In 1944 the McNair Committee commented on the need for youth workers to act as 'guides, philosophers and friends' (HMSO 1944: 103) to young people. The contention here is that youth workers should provide a steer for young people through the philosophical enquiry into the nature, significance and interrelationship of their values and beliefs, based on a relationship of true friendship – wanting for someone what one thinks good for his or her sake and not for one's own (Aristotle 1987). Indeed the nature and quality of this relationship is crucial since the moral and intellectual activities involved in such a philosophical enquiry are activities necessarily shared with others who are not only friends but who are also 'themselves morally good persons' (Cooper 1980: 331). Therefore, in order to engage in this philosophical enquiry youth workers need to possess the knowledge, skills and dispositions which enable them, following Aristotle (1987) to: *deliberate* about what is good, not in particular respects but in terms of what is conducive to the good life generally (ibid.: 191); and *choose* to do the virtuous thing for its own sake (ibid.: 501).

However, being a morally good person is not simply a question of behaving in certain ways. Being a morally good or virtuous person requires the individual to choose to act in certain ways based on a *disposition* towards certain ideals. Virtue is a disposition of character which helps to determine, in different situations, what action one will want to take (Williams 1993: 9). Virtue asks not 'what should I do?' but 'what would the just or benevolent, or trust-worthy or courageous (that is, virtuous) person do?' In addition, virtue is a disposition towards feeling as well as action:

> The moral person is seen as one whose moral choices reflect reasoned and deliberate judgements that ensure justice be accorded each person while maintaining a passionate concern for the well-being and care of each individual.
>
> (Brabeck 1993: 48)

Virtuous workers therefore bring integrity to their relationships with young people. Credible workers establish their 'moral authority' through the demonstration of behaviour consistent with their espoused values (Jeffs and Smith 1996: 52). These relationships do not, however, exist in a vacuum. They have a context which neces-sarily includes: utilising the materials of typical social situations (Dewey 1961) through engagement with young people's real lives – as opposed to systematised exercises about imagined incidents or situations – and a genuine appreciation of their view of the world, their accounts of their experiences, their dilemmas and conflicts. It also includes 'conversations' which according to Jeffs and Smith (1996: 30) involve:

- concern – in being *with* our partners in conversation; engaging with them;
- trust – taking what others say on faith;
- respect – mutual regard;
- appreciation – valuing the other's qualities;
- affection – a feeling with and for our partners;
- hope – faith in the inherent value of education.

Indeed it is through such reciprocal relationships, engagement and conversation that young people can best be supported to become aware of their values; gain the critical abilities needed to mediate those values; and grow in their ability to make decisions which can be sustained through committed action.

However, creating such a context does not come easy. It requires the worker to understand 'what sort of person he himself [*sic*] is, what his needs are and what his beliefs and values are' (Davies and Gibson 1967: 186). This necessarily involves the worker in:

> a careful, philosophical reflection upon what it means to be a person, how development as a person is inextricably linked with a form of social life, and where moral values and ideas are presupposed in both.
>
> (Pring 1984: 167)

Indeed, the McNair Committee (HMSO 1944: 106) commented that:

> A well-informed philosophy of life, which may or may not be professedly religious, is most necessary to the youth leader; indeed, it is not easy to conceive of a successful youth leader without it.

On participation and autonomy

If youth work is fundamentally concerned with the development of young people's values and specifically their moral deliberations and education then it is clear that such a process requires young people's participation. But this participation is more than young people simply taking part or having a say in the 'development of self-programming groups' (HMSO 1960: 63); more than their active participation in the learning process (HMSO 1969); more than giving them a 'sense of belonging, a sense of identity, and the skills, confidence and assurance needed to participate not only in his [*sic*] club or organisation but also in society at large' (HMSO 1982: 38). Participation represents more than the 'degree' of young people's involvement (Treseder 1997: 7). Certainly it requires involvement, engagement and the encouragement of young people to be 'creators rather than consumers of situations' (Smith 1994: 64).

However, the process could only be described as participative if three prior conditions are met:

- First, that the *intention* as well as the process is made explicit to young people.
- Second, that young people engage in deliberation and discussion which helps them to clarify their understanding and gain a *real* sense of what is involved.
- Third, that young people give their *conscious* and informed consent to engage – not in the arts weekend, health discussion or camping trip – but in the process of moral philosophising.

If, and only if, these conditions are met could young people be said to be 'partners in learning and decision-making' (NYA 1997). For participation is not an absent minded exercise; and neither can it be hidden or coerced. Indeed, participation in the processes described here can only be meaningful if it is grounded in young people's informed, conscious consent. This is because the process of moral education is necessarily open to examination and negotiation. And this is what sets it apart from other approaches which could better be described as moral training or, in other instances, moral indoctrination. For central to the educative process is the capacity for rational judgement by autonomous human beings – that is, people capable of acting in accordance with reason and from their own free will, voluntarily as opposed to acting 'under compulsion or from ignorance' (Aristotle 1987: 66).

'Increasing young people's maturity for their own society' (Davies and Gibson 1967: 96) or the 'transition to responsible adulthood' (NYA 1997) could therefore be understood as the growth towards autonomy – not only in the sense of acting from free will but also according to Pring (1984: 74) in terms of:

- a disposition towards increasingly questioning taken-for-granted attitudes, assumptions and beliefs;
- an increasing integration of the values and purposes that permeate one's actions and relationships;

- a sense of one's own value and identity through different situations, circumstances and pressures.

The youth work process becomes the process of self examination through which young people increasingly integrate their values, actions and identity. Indeed, in discussing the purpose of youth work, Smith (1988: xii) suggests that:

> practitioners should set out to enable individuals to autonomously pursue their own well-being. In particular they should seek to enlarge young people's understanding of their own well-being so that they may weigh their own needs with those of others, help them to display civic courage, and enable them to gain the knowledge, skills and disposition necessary to think and act politically.

Well-being (Aristotle 1987) is understood to include: autonomy – free reasoned choices; practical wisdom – the ability to deliberate about what is good; self respect – including a sense of shame. Indeed, according to Mencius (1970: 129), 'Only when a man will not do some things is he capable of doing great things'.

Learning to develop 'civic courage' is described as involving critical engagement in the learning process, the ability to think critically, the ability to reason, learning what is 'good' and what values are central to human well-being, and learning about the 'structural and ideological forces which influence and restrict' our lives (Smith 1988: 114).

Participation is therefore much more than simply 'taking part' or 'having a say' or even being party to decision-making. Participation involves a process of conscious critical engagement and committed self reflection. However, this is not to be understood simply as a one dimensional exercise in purging the self for:

> Unless I am able to analyse the unconscious aspects of the society in which I live, I cannot know who I am, because I do not know which part of me is *not* me.
>
> (Fromm 1993: 78)

The youth work process is three-dimensional since it seeks to enable young people to become conscious of and able to deliberate about: the sort of people they want to be; the sort of relationships and interactions they want to have; and the sort of society they want to live in. In choosing to engage, young people accept the inevitable consequence of having to question not only themselves but their relationships, the structure of their lives and the society in which they live. In doing so they are brought face-to-face with the structural inequalities and institutionalised oppressions which advantage some groups of people at the expense of others and which tip the balance of power in ways which act to dominate rather than liberate.

Empowerment

Young people's participation becomes empowering by virtue of their increasing critical engagement and ability to act in accordance with reason. That is, their empowerment lies in their growth towards autonomy and their capacity to function well 'as a person, not as an instrument' (Fromm 1993: 117).

This offers a different emphasis from other definitions of empowerment. For example, within human resource management and organisational development, empowerment is seen, essentially, as a way of increasing the performance standards of staff; a way of getting people to become more effective in their jobs. Stewart (1994: 2) writes:

> Empowerment seeks to eliminate all the unnecessary rules, procedures, standing orders etc. which actually stand between the organisation and its goals. The aim is to remove as many restrictions as possible in order to unblock the organisation and the people who work in it, liberating them from unnecessary limitations which slow their response and constrain their action.

The motivation is clearly directed towards the benefits for the organisation. But the idea that people can be 'liberated' from limitations which 'constrain their action' is an idea central to discussions about empowerment within social/community work where the demand is for the elimination of the barriers which obstruct social justice, respectful treatment and equal rights (Friedmann 1992). Indeed, empowerment within social–community work is understood predominantly in terms of powerlessness and oppression. O'Brien and Whitmore (quoted in Morley 1991: 14) define empowerment as:

an interactive process through which less powerful people experience personal and social change, enabling them to achieve influence over the organisations and institutions which affect their lives and the communities in which they live.

Similarly, Barry (1996: 3) defines empowerment as:

the end result of participative practices where each participant gains control and/or influence over issues of concern to them.

Not surprisingly, the development of practice has tended to focus on empowerment as processes and techniques for changing power relations (Dalrymple and Burke 1995; Braye and Preston-Shoot 1995; Adams 1996). However, whilst the development of structures for decision-making, partnership and power-sharing provide a framework for empowerment they do not necessarily create its substance. Indeed, it is possible for such initiatives to become simply 'islands of empowerment' in a wider sea of oppression (Stevenson and Parsloe 1993: 14) – particular episodes, at a particular time, about a particular issue in people's lives. This is not to suggest that such initiatives are unworthy or unimportant. Such developments are critical to challenging and changing the material circumstances of people's lives. Nonetheless:

the true focus of revolutionary change is never merely the oppressive situations which we seek to escape, but that piece of the oppressor which is planted deep within each of us, and which knows only the oppressors' tactics, the oppressors' relationships.

(Lorde 1984: 123)

So when we think of empowerment as: 'supporting young people to understand and act on the personal, social and political issues which affect their lives, the lives of others and the communities of which they are a part' (NYB 1990: 16), the suggestion is not only that young people be supported to oppose the external forces of oppression but also, and importantly, that they have opportunities to examine the internal bridles and perceived powerlessness which underpin their sense of self and guide their actions in the world. For the essential basis of empowerment lies not in the development of power-sharing structures but in the reclaiming of oneself as fully human, fully intelligent and fully powerful. And it is from this place that we venture into the world to make our contribution and to transform it.

Conclusions: on reflection and practice

This chapter advances five main arguments. First, youth work's fundamental purpose is to support young people's moral deliberations and learning. This involves enabling them to explore their values, interrogate the principles of their own moral judgements and make reasoned choices that can be sustained through committed action. Second, such a process is neither mindless nor mechanistic since it is based on the capacity for rational judgement by autonomous human beings concerned about what they are in their relationships with others. Third, the context which best supports young people's moral deliberations and learning includes: reciprocal relationships with morally good persons; engagement with young people's real lives; and 'conversations' which enable them to develop their ability to think critically. Fourth, participation in such a process can only be meaningful if young people give their conscious and informed consent to engage. Fifth, the real powerhouse of empowerment lies not in the development of power-sharing structures but rather in each individual's ability to transcend the internalised lies, myths and misinformation which keep us corralled in our own sense of powerlessness – women, men, black, white, gay, lesbian, heterosexual, working class, middle class......

This, however is not new for youth work. Rather it represents a return to first principles – to the idea of social education – attention to the social context of young people's development not as citizenship or life skills' training; not because they are marginalised, alienated or excluded; not because they *cause* problems or *are* problems but simply because they are in the process of creating themselves.

In accepting the challenge which this offers, workers must be prepared to overcome any sense of selfishness; uncover the roots of their fears, sense of powerlessness, distrust of people; commit themselves to the world outside of their own ego; and, importantly, change their practice (Fromm 1993: 119). For the real challenge is how to develop a youth work practice which enables young people to gain the critical and emotional capacities necessary to engage in moral philosophising and as a result, take charge of themselves as positive rational agents as opposed to powerless victims.

Bibliography

Adams, R. (1996) *Social Work and Empowerment*, London: Macmillan.

Aristotle (1987) *The Nicomachean Ethics*, trans. J. Welldon, New York: Prometheus Books.

Barrow, R. (1981) *The Philosophy of Schooling*, Brighton: Wheatsheaf Books.

Barry, M. (1996) 'The empowering process', *Youth and Policy* 54: 1–12.

Booton, F. (1985) *Studies in Social Education: Vol. 1. 1860–1890*, Hove: Benfield Press.

Brabeck, M. (1993) 'Moral judgement: theory and research on differences between males and females' in M. Larrabee (ed.) *An Ethic of Care*, London: Routledge.

Braye, S. and Preston-Shoot, M (1995) *Empowering Practice in Social Work*, Buckingham: Open University Press.

Brew, J. (1957) *Youth & Youth Groups*, London: Faber and Faber.

Brown, H. and Draper, M. (1997) *Occupational and Functional Mapping of Youth Work*, London: DfEE.

Coleman, J. (1992) 'The nature of adolescence' in J. Coleman and C. Warren-Adamson (eds) *Youth Policy in the 1990s*, London: Routledge.

Cooper, J. (1980) 'Aristotle on friendship' in A. Rorty (ed.) *Essays on Aristotle's 'Ethics'*, Los Angeles: University of California Press.

Dalrymple, J. and Burke, B. (1995) *Anti-Oppressive Practice: Social Care and the Law*, Buckingham: Open University Press.

Davies, B. and Gibson, A. (1967) *The social education of the adolescent*, London: University of London Press.

Dewey, J. (1961) *Democracy and Education: An Introduction to the Philosophy of Education*, New York: Macmillan.

Eggleston, J. (1976) *Adolescence and Community*, London: Edward Arnold.

Friedmann, J. (1992) *Empowerment: The Politics of Alternative Development*, Cambridge MA: Blackwell.

Fromm, E. (1993) *The Art of Being*, London: Constable.

Goleman, D. (1996) *Emotional Intelligence – Why It Can Matter More Than IQ*, London: Bloomsbury.

Guide Association (1996) *Inside Out: Values and Attitudes Training For Those Involved In Personal Development*, London: Guide Association.

HMSO (1940) *The Challenge of Youth (Circular 1516)*, London: HMSO (now available in *Documents of Historical Importance*, 1982, National Youth Bureau).

——— (1944) *Teachers and Youth Leaders: Report of the Committee appointed by the Board of Education to consider the Supply, Recruitment and Training of Teachers and Youth Leaders*, (The McNair Report), London: HMSO.

——— (1960) *The Youth Service in England and Wales* (The Albemarle Report), London: HMSO.

—— (1969) *Youth and Community Work in the '70s* (The Milson Fairbairn Report) London: HMSO.

—— (1982) *Experience and Participation: Report of the Review Group on the Youth Service in England* (The Thompson Report) London: HMSO.

Jeffs, T. and Smith, M. (1990) *Young People, Inequality and Youth Work*, London: Macmillan.

—— (1996) *Informal Education: Conversation, Democracy and Learning*, Derby: Education Now Publishing Co-operative.

Kleinig, J. (1982) *Philosophical Issues in Education*, London: Croom Helm.

Leighton, J. (1972) *The Principles and Practice of Youth and Community Work*, London: Chester House Publications.

Lewes, J. (1996) 'Values education in a youth work curriculum' in W. Robb (ed), *Values Education: The Contribution of Some Voluntary Youth Organisations*, Aberdeen: Centre for Alleviating Social Problems through Values Education.

Lorde, A. (1984) *Sister Outsider*, Freedom CA: Crossing Press.

Maud, J. (1951) in *Youth Service Tomorrow*, report of meeting arranged by King George's Jubilee Trust and held at Ashridge, 27–30 April 1951: 13.

Mencius (1970) trans. D. Lau, Harmondsworth: Penguin.

Morley, L. (1991) 'Towards a pedagogy for empowerment in community and youth work training', *Youth and Policy* 35: 14–19.

National Forum for Values in Education and the Community (1996) *Consultation on Values in Education and the Community*, London: SCAA.

National Youth Agency (1997) *Youth Service Statement of Purpose*, Leicester: NYA.

National Youth Bureau (1990) *Towards a Core Curriculum: The Next Step* (Papers, prepared by Kerry Young for Second Ministerial Conference for the Youth Service) Leicester: NYB.

NCVYS (1997) *Clipboard*, Issue 3, London: National Council for Voluntary Youth Services.

Pring, R. (1984) *Personal and Social Education in the Curriculum*, London: Hodder and Stoughton.

Raths, L., Harmin, M. and Simon, S. (1966) *Values and Teaching*, Columbus Ohio: Merrill.

Robb, W. (ed.) (1996a) *Values Education: The Contribution of Some Voluntary Youth Organisations*, Aberdeen: CAVE.

—— (1996b) *Values Education for More Effective: Moral Education, Religious Education, Citizenship Education, Health Education, Sex Education, Environmental Education, Alcohol Education, Multicultural Education and Personal and Social Education*, Aberdeen: CAVE.

Rokeach, M. (1973) *The Nature of Human Values*, New York: Free Press.

Smith, M. (1988) *Developing Youth Work*, Milton Keynes: Open University Press.

—— (1994) *Local Education*, Milton Keynes: Open University Press.

Stevenson, O. and Parsloe, P. (1993) *Community Care and Empowerment*, York: Joseph Rowntree Foundation.

Stewart, A. (1994) *Empowering People*, London: Institute of Management/Pitman.

Thompson, N. (1993) *Anti-Discriminatory Practice*, London: Macmillan.

Treseder, P. (1997) *Empowering Children and Young People: Training Manual*, London: Save The Children.

Williams, B. (1993) *Ethics and the Limits of Philosophy*, Hammersmith: Fontana.

YMCA (1987) *The YMCA in Focus*, London: YMCA.

Youth Advisory Council (1945) *The Purpose and Content of the Youth Service*, London: HMSO.

Ymlaen (1997) Magazine of the Wales Youth Agency, no. 8, Summer.

6

YOUTH WORKERS AS CONTROLLERS

Issues of method and purpose

Tony Jeffs and Sarah Banks

Introduction

Most commentators seem to agree that a control agenda is becoming more explicit and more dominant within youth work in recent years. However, there is some debate about whether youth workers should embrace this agenda as providing a socially recognised and valued rationale for the work, or whether it runs contrary to the values of youth work and corrupts its essential nature. In order to explore the issues involved in this debate more fully we will look at what is meant by 'control' in youth work.

'Youth workers as controllers' can have several different meanings. The current debate about control in youth work has generally focused around whether or not control, in the sense of diverting or preventing young people from activities considered harmful, should be regarded, and indeed promoted, as a core purpose of the work. There are some who argue strongly that youth work can make a big impact in this area and should not be shy about accepting funding explicitly for such targeted work and demonstrating its impact (France and Wiles 1996, 1997; Smith and Paylor 1997). Others argue against such a position, claiming it is incompatible with an educational purpose for the work: it threatens the voluntary and universal nature of youth provision; marginalises those not regarded as problematic; and works to an externally-defined agenda rather than a local analysis of young people's needs (Jeffs and Smith 1994, 1996a).

There is another sense in which youth workers might be regarded as controllers which reflects debates of the 1970s and 1980s about social control in welfare work. This position would acknowledge that the core purpose of the work is education, but would argue that even education is or can be controlling, and that the purpose of education is in fact to socialise young people to fit into society and accept its norms. Although this brand of 'radical pessimism' has less purchase now, it is worth revisiting briefly to test its relevance to current debates.

The third sense of youth workers as controllers relates to methods and styles of practice, rather than purpose. If we regard the first two of these as 'practice for control', then this third is about 'control in practice'. This is less talked about now than in the past – having connotations of discipline, autocratic leadership, rules and punishment. Yet some degree of control on the part of youth workers is essential in order to create an appropriate learning environment, promote equality of opportunity and ensure the safety and well-being of young people. It is around this issue that many of the biggest day-to-day ethical dilemmas arise for workers: for example, how much influence or control should they exert without compromising the freedom and responsibility of the young people?

In order to shed light on this topic of youth workers as controllers we will begin by exploring control in practice, moving on to look at practice for control through education and through prevention/diversion.

Control in practice

Early practitioners generally held control and good discipline to be the key to effective youth work. As one text warned novices:

> firm discipline is absolutely essential. More well-meant efforts for lads have failed through lack of ability to maintain good discipline than from any other cause.
>
> (Bickerdike 1926: 16)

Yet youth workers also recognised the dangers of excessive discipline and were concerned to differentiate youth clubs and youth workers from schools and teachers (Jephcott 1942; Russell and Russell 1932; Secretan 1931). Most schools were, it seems, obsessed with order and collective management. As the following account of schooling in the late nineteenth century demonstrates, keeping control was the prime task of the teacher, fuelling repeated admonition:

Such phrases as 'Don't talk', 'Don't fidget', 'Don't worry', 'Don't ask questions', 'Don't make a noise', 'Don't make a mess', 'Don't do this thing', 'Don't do that thing', are ever falling from [the teacher's] lips. And they are supplemented with such positive instructions as: 'Sit still', 'Stand on the form', 'Hold yourself up', 'Hands behind backs', 'Hands on heads', 'Eyes on the blackboard'.

(Davin 1996: 122)

Ultimately such instructions were enforced by recourse to the strap, slap and cane. Schools, especially those provided for the poor, were generally violent, dismal, boring places where attendance was often only secured by threats of legal action against parents and the incarceration of persistent truants (Hurt 1979). Within such an environment uniformity rather than creativity became the more desirable attribute. For, like imagination, the latter were 'inconvenient to the teacher' (Russell 1932: 95).

Compulsion was never an option for youth work. Therefore workers knew from the onset that to make an impact meant cultivating ways of working which distanced them from schoolteachers. According to Hannah More, possibly the first modern youth worker, this meant learning to teach not by dull rote but dialogue 'through animated conversation and lively discussion' (quoted in Collingwood and Collingwood 1990: 106). Baden-Powell also stressed the need to offer radically dissimilar approaches to those employed by schools in order to hold the allegiance of young people. Be prepared, he told his followers, to 'use as bait the food the fish likes...to hold out something that really attracts and interests them' (1908: 271). Youth workers, in particular, looked to group work (Scouts and Guides called it the patrol system) rather than classroom instruction as the means 'to develop people' (Kingman and Sidman 1935: 19). They placed substantial emphasis on the need to foster friendship between the adults and young people, self-discipline rather than imposed order, activities rather than passive instruction. Consequently, youth work acquired a distinctive vocabulary which helped to distinguish it from school-based education. Leaders, not teachers, organised the learning; sessions, not periods or classes, divided up the time; and participants were members, even clients, never students or pupils. Nevertheless, according to Baden Powell (1908: 272) it was still important that 'discipline and good order should be kept inside the room, and neatness insisted on'.

Nowadays the literature largely eschews the topic of discipline.

Managers similarly refrain from issuing the sort of instructions Baden Powell and his ilk handed down to a previous generation of workers. Yet, although the topic is less openly discussed, contemporary workers cannot evade it. Like progressive educators in the school sector they must continually wrestle with the problem of unearthing ways of managing and controlling the learning experience without resorting to harsh and inappropriate stratagems, and to discover approaches whereby neither subject nor teacher dominate yet enable learning to take place.

Workers such as Phillips had an intuitive belief that:

> collective discipline fails to develop the individual and as a result fails to bring forward the right kind of leader. It produces the drill-sergeant type as opposed to the imaginative Scoutmaster.
>
> (quoted by Gate 1933: 52)

It was a view which seemed to be confirmed by highly influential 'scientific' research undertaken by Lewin and his associates in the 1930s (Lewin, Lippitt and White 1939). This contrasted the impact of what they termed the autocratic, democratic and laissez-faire styles of leadership within boys' club settings. Their results strongly suggested autocracy was generally accompanied either by rebellion or by submission on the part of the boys. It was highly productive when the autocratic leader was present, but destructive behaviour was common in his absence. Democratic leadership was, they argued, more 'task-orientated, cooperative...friendly' (ibid.: 278), encouraging independent behaviour especially when the leader was not in attendance. Laissez-faire leadership did least for productivity, and was often accompanied by intra-group hostility. In almost every case the democratic style was preferred by the group.

However, that is not to say the democratic style is appropriate in all situations, nor should it be assumed that a democratic worker never uses formal methods. Libertarian and progressive educators have always found it necessary to adopt formal methods to teach certain subjects (Shotton 1993), just as youth workers and informal educators must when working with young people in 'dangerous' settings such as canoeing or horse riding. Equally a desire to eschew the formal and didactic amongst youth workers may help explain why they concentrate on educating through the medium of art, drama, environmental issues and the like where 'projects can develop without too much artificiality' (Peters 1959: 129). In the process they leave subjects less amenable to informal and conversational methods to others.

Yet, however great the desire to foster imagination and teach via 'novelty, excitement, fun, a chance to explore new things' (Jephcott 1942: 67), youth workers have to exercise a measure of control over the learning experience. They have to temper their optimism that somehow the natural curiosity of young people will lead them naturally towards learning things of educational value. By challenging those they work with regarding 'their certitudes' (Freire 1997: 83) it is possible to extract educational outputs from almost any setting or experience. However constantly demanding that young people justify their opinions and behaviour is a technique which has limited mileage. Therefore it is essential workers construct opportunities for learning by initiating events, organising visits and distributing materials with the intention of stimulating conversation and directing the attention of young people towards the consideration of particular topics and subjects. Such interventions will by their very nature seek to encourage certain beliefs, attitudes and outcomes rather than others. As teachers and educators, rather than mere facilitators, youth workers engage in the process of selection and in so doing aim to manage and control the learning of those young people with whom they work. The educational aims may be hidden behind a veil of activity and the involvement of the young people voluntary. Nevertheless, youth workers are exercising control as much as the traditional teacher. Moral and ethical education may not involve memorising rules and procedures, but it does involve acquiring 'habits of conduct in the same way we acquire our native language' (Oakeshott 1962: 62) – that is, by sharing experiences with people who behave in certain ways. Therefore, for exactly the same reasons that schoolteachers must justify the content of their lessons, so youth workers must be prepared to defend their interventions – to explain why they shape and manage the learning of others in particular ways.

Control in practice is part of youth workers' responsibility to ensure an appropriate learning environment is created. To this end workers and their managers or agencies make rules and plan programmes and activities (often in conjunction with young people). This is essentially about setting the scene for the work. During the course of the work occasions may also arise when workers may have to control or 'restrain' the young people they work with. The kinds of reasons workers may give for intervening to control the context of the work or the behaviour of particular young people include:

1 Educational challenge

Workers may intervene to maintain balance within the programme, using their professional judgement. Peters (1963) talks of the duty of the educator to 'initiate' young people into areas of knowledge they would not otherwise encounter. For example, a group of young people planning a series of activities may have chosen all sports-related activities in a nearby leisure centre. The worker may start a discussion about why they made these choices, and suggest a trip to a city farm or outdoor rock-climbing to broaden their horizons.

2 Equality of access

Promotion of equality has often been viewed as one of the key aims of youth work practice. One of the ways in which this may be denied is if a particular project or centre works only with a small group of people, effectively excluding others who might benefit. For example, workers may intervene in a male-dominated centre which has a reputation for aggression and toughness in order to create an atmosphere more conducive to encouraging the participation of young women who are currently not members and are, in effect, being denied access to facilities.

3 Equality of treatment

Workers may intervene to prevent young people victimising, bullying or harassing other individuals or groups. For example, a group of young Asian women participating in a project may face continuous racial jibes and taunts which workers have a duty to challenge. The issue for the worker is when and how to challenge constructively and ensure those doing the taunting not only stop, but understand why it is wrong. Workers may sometimes have to exclude certain young people from a centre, event or meeting if their behaviour is unacceptable, because allowing them to stay, or giving them a lot of time and attention, would disadvantage others.

4 Promotion of welfare

Workers have a duty to their employers and parents to ensure the safety and well-being of participants in specific ways. They may also judge they have a general duty to protect young people from harming themselves or others, particularly those who are vulnerable. This they may do, for example, through stopping a fight, or banning drugs and alcohol on premises. This kind of intervention may be straightforward in a case of obvious danger or infringement of a rule the worker believes in. In other cases there may be a fine line between respecting young people's freedom to make their own choices (including mistakes) and unwarranted interference and parentalism (see Banks 1997: 222).

Practice for control

Control through education

Quite often reference is made to youth work as a form of social control, meaning that it is about socialising young people into modes of behaviour and responsible citizenship so they fit into society. This is quite consistent with its educational purpose and in some ways, given our discussion above, it is difficult to dispute this claim. However, most youth workers would not identify this as the core purpose of their work. For there is a sense in which all those working in welfare occupations, including educators, are inevitably involved in transmitting prevailing values and norms, although some adopt a more critical approach than others. Youth workers would tend to stress the development of critical thinking, questioning, and extending young people's choices. They might talk more of participating in society than fitting in, about fostering democracy rather than responsibility (Smith 1994). In so doing they would inevitably endeavour to transform the focus of debate about control from one which has largely been centred on how society might better manage and control the behaviour of young people and others into one more concerned with how individuals as citizens, rather than subjects, might more forcefully manage the state, those institutions they engage with – such as schools in the case of young people – and their social environment.

It is important for workers to be aware that neither the work they are doing nor the role of an educator are neutral; that education can be a force for challenge and change or for fortifying the status quo. Most workers are clear that youth work is not about indoctrination or brainwashing. Arguably these would not be defined as education in the strict sense. Although there is no doubt that what passes for, or has passed itself off, as 'education' has frequently had such goals in mind. The potential for the misuse of the role of educator is great – as Green's chapter discusses in relation to religious conversion. Increasingly, though, the danger within both the formal and informal sectors appears to emanate not from rogue educators seeking to indoctrinate young people and convert them to a particular religious or political viewpoint, but from a highly centralised state determined to restrict the educational experience to what it deems useful, worthwhile and safe. Within the formal sector the government has relentlessly moved from imposing a National Curriculum, without even a token consultation with teachers, to the production of national textbooks in English, maths, design and technology, science, history and geography. This is an imposition defended by the minister responsible as a means of freeing teachers so they might 'concentrate on teaching' (Speech to the National Union of Teachers, 13 April 1998). This approach, by denying the teacher and the student the opportunity to assemble a curriculum, to even negotiate sequence effectively, reduces the role of the former to that of an instructor.

Youth workers still retain far greater freedom from bureaucratic control than their colleagues in the school sector. They largely retain the ability to choose both what and how they wish to teach. This autonomy allows them, if they so wish, to create what Haynes terms a 'community of enquiry' (1998: 133). Space to work with young people constructing programmes and creating experiences of shared communal learning which can respond directly to the expressed needs of the participants. Top-down models which treat young people and youth workers as a means to an end are difficult to implement. Youth work that takes place in small units or on the street is not easily monitored, whilst the voluntary nature of the affiliation makes the measurement of outcomes highly problematic. Growing pressure to formularise youth work, create chains of command and produce identifiable outcomes are slowly eroding the capacity of workers to structure communities of enquiry. Funders are seeking to impose conditions which require workers to show they have reduced offending, anti-social behaviour or risk activities in a given area. Prepackaged programmes or 'curriculum units' are also increasingly being provided by some employers who make their use mandatory. Such changes, like those enforced upon schoolteachers, may be opposed by educators and young people alike, but the pressures to conform in the name of efficiency and effectiveness are immense. Punitive financial penalties, in particular, impose either conformity or a requirement that workers lie about outcomes and the work undertaken to secure a continuation of funding. This fosters an approach to the work where 'getting through the programme becomes the end' and to which the understanding of the young person becomes 'subordinated' (ibid.: 49).

Control by diversion and prevention

The third sense of youth work as control has a more direct relationship to the maintenance of public order – the prevention and diversion of young people from trouble, crime and causing disturbance. This version of youth work as control would regard the achievement of such outcomes either as the core purpose, or one of the main purposes of youth work. Using youth work methods – informal educational processes – the aim is to reduce or prevent truancy, offending, teenage pregnancies, or any other of the myriad of social problems thought to be caused by 'out-of-control' young people. Recently there has been a growth of youth work in these fields, with many specialised projects being established which stress this approach either in their titles or in their stated aims of 'diversion from crime', 'alternatives to custody' or 'truancy reduction'. This has led to a debate as to whether youth work agencies should participate in such projects.

Youth crime prevention work is a particularly interesting example, with some commentators suggesting that the youth service should 'welcome opportunities to become involved more explicitly in preventing youth crime, that there is encouraging evidence that it can do so successfully' (Smith and Paylor 1997: 17) and that youth workers 'should see this as a "window of opportunity" to create a clear role for themselves in future initiatives' (France and Wiles 1997: 13). On the other hand, Jeffs and Smith (1994: 25) warn against the gradual replacement of the educational orientation of most youth work initiatives by control, identifying a drift towards a 'new authoritarianism' forcing workers increasingly into 'modes of intervention located within a tradition of behaviour modification rather than education for autonomy and choice'.

Both these positions seem somewhat extreme. There certainly is a danger of the new authoritarianism pushing youth work towards the control end of the spectrum of work. Funding and work is increasingly targeted on those perceived to be most 'at risk' or problematic (see chapters by Mizen; Jeffs and Smith). Yet it is interesting that accounts of work funded specifically with a crime prevention remit such as the Youth Action Schemes (France and Wiles 1996; Smith and Paylor 1997) do not describe a practice using behaviour modification techniques, manipulation or authoritarian rules. Youth workers, it seems, recognise they are not police, probation officers or social workers. They know that, if they embrace the crime control agenda too overtly and directly, there is a danger they will cease to be youth workers, and that they will be tempted, or pushed, to use a range of methods and techniques not usually associated with youth work to achieve the outcomes required by their sponsors or employers. By doing that, they risk not only losing whatever precarious identity they hold as youth workers, but risk failing in the task set by their funders or sponsors. The reason why youth work may be successful in working with young people categorised as 'at risk' is precisely because it does so in an informal and participative way; it tends to work alongside and with young people and listen to their concerns and needs. As soon as the workers become over-preoccupied with achieving prescribed outputs and monitoring and evaluating their results, their primary focus is distracted from the young people themselves and their work can become less effective. This is not to say that workers should not evaluate the impact of their work, but it may explain some of their reluctance to do so.

France and Wiles (1996: 26), in their evaluation of the Youth Action Scheme projects (which specifically funded local authority youth services to undertake work with young people to reduce the risk of them becoming involved in crime), report that only three of the fifty projects they investigated were able to show the impact their work was having on young people's involvement in crime. The failure of the youth workers to develop adequate systems of monitoring and evaluation is linked to inadequate training and resistance to aspects of the scheme which 'brought the youth service closer to an overtly controlling role' (Smith and Paylor 1997: 25). However, maybe it is less the case that youth workers are inadequately skilled in evaluation and the manipulation of statistics, or that they are 'reluctant heroes' in the war against crime, but more that their honesty obliges them to acknowledge that reductions in crime are at best a fortuitous and desirable by-product of their work. Their own accounts of their work speak instead of building relationships based on mutual trust, facilitating the learning process, and engaging in challenging and confidence-building activities (ibid.: 20–1).

A demarcation line, however ill-defined at times, does exist between those employed to control the criminal activities of young people, such as crime prevention officers or security officers patrolling a shopping precinct, and a detached youth worker. All three may operate in the same locality, focus their attention on young people, seek out their company and engage in conversation with them. However their reasons for doing so vary enormously. For the first two the purpose is to prevent the young people from committing crime. Therefore, they have no professional interest in those who 'behave' except as potential deviants or purveyors of information about criminal peers. Youth workers operate according to different criteria. For them, any decision to focus attention on one segment of the youth population in the area must be justified according to need. They must be able to justify their grounds for targeting on the basis of a professional judgement which takes full account of who will benefit most from their intervention and where the greatest need resides. They can no more justify working with one segment because they are more likely to misbehave than on the grounds that they enjoy their company more.

The second reason why targeting those misbehaving jeopardises the distinctiveness of youth work relates to the educational process itself. Although youth workers may run programmes and initiate activities, these are not their prime purpose. They are the means whereby opportunities for dialogue and conversation can be engendered. Via these the worker can express concern for young people, indicate interest in them as persons, display trust and respect and show that they value them as individuals. However, such relationships must be open and honest. Dialogue, as opposed to instruction, requires the worker to treat young people as worthy of respect. Respect can be regarded as an 'active sympathy' towards another human being (Downie and Telfer 1969: 1980). In the Kantian sense, this human being is a person who has desires and hopes and is capable of making choices and therefore should never be treated simply as a means to our ends (Kant 1964: 32–3). Whatever the differences in age, income or background, the worker has to be with that person, rather than seeking merely to act upon them. This is crucial. If the worker enters into dialogue with the desire merely to act upon those they are working with, then they are perceiving them as an object rather than a person. When this is the case then it is wholly or partially closed to interaction (Jeffs and Smith 1996b).

In the absence of mutual respect, genuine dialogue – when individuals share ideas and are simultaneously open to the views of others – ceases to be tenable. For mutual respect cannot long survive within relationships where one party holds itself morally, intellectually and ethically superior to the other. Within such a climate informal educators would be unable to justify a modus operandi based on a belief that they are engaging with equals. Their faith in the potential of education via dialogue and conversation would consequently be shown to have been profoundly misplaced. They would be left with no choice but to opt for more formal and structured modes of intervention – programmes of instruction based on the sort of implicit contract club and centre workers often made, where they offer 'clients' access to leisure facilities or welfare services in return for participation in morally improving programmes. This type of approach is one where the ends (better behaviour) would be used to justify the means (formal contracts).

The application of youth work techniques to crime prevention work is not something most workers would intrinsically find unacceptable. Indeed, as an alternative to military-style policing operations, the arbitrary exclusion of young people from public space and the use of gratuitous violence against potential offenders to discourage their presence, it would be an attractive option. Further, if their introduction precipitates a decline in offending behaviour then this is something again which most would surely welcome. However, the question remains whether adoption of specific techniques and styles of practice (informal educational methods) can transform crime management or prevention programmes into youth work. If the core purpose of the work ceases to be education, and the values relating to respect, equality of opportunity and participation are lost, then it is doubtful.

Yet there is no doubt that at a micro-level of day-to-day practice, most workers on such projects are still doing what we would recognise as youth work and are relating to young people as educators. While at a macro-level, the policy and funding framework within which they are doing this has a utilitarian stress on outcomes relating to the control and management of dangerous and threatening youth. State welfare workers have always had to manage the tension between developing autonomy and control – and as long as autonomy at the micro-level showed up as control at the macro-level, everybody was satisfied. However, workers are now being asked to prove this link. This threatens the educational purpose and approach of their work. They are being asked to make explicit what was hitherto accepted as implicit. They are being asked to state as a core purpose what was once regarded as a desirable by-product. The policy and funding framework is no longer a rather distant set of limits which can be left to managers, but threatens to become intertwined with the everyday work. What was once experienced as a cocoon, seems now more like a spider's web. Before they become too hopelessly enmeshed, youth workers and youth work managers need to stop and take serious stock of where the silken trail will lead them.

The question as to whether the youth service and youth workers should eschew work specifically focusing on changing the behaviour of 'problematic' groups and keep their hands 'clean' is not a simple one to answer. It will depend on the outcomes expected of the work and the extent to which workers may have to target their work and use alien techniques. Mounting governmental concern relating to an assumed rise in levels of juvenile offending and the appearance of what has been dubbed an 'underclass' has led to a marked shift in the allocation of funding to projects which claim to manage and control 'disaffected youth' (Jeffs and Smith 1994; Jeffs 1997a; 1997b). As is noted in the chapter on funding by Jeffs and Smith, the growing use of targeted funding poses a dilemma for youth workers. It is creating more jobs for them and providing resources. However, in return it requires youth workers to set aside their professional judgement regarding with whom they ought to work. Where the focus is upon control, then inevitably those who pose the least threat will receive the least attention. This will mean the neglect of work with those who tend to be less visible, less trouble-some and less demanding. Where does this leave work with young women (except as potential teenage mothers or drug users), with lesbian, gay or bisexual young people (except as potential victims of AIDS) or with young people with disabilities, for example? These are serious ethical issues for workers as well as policy makers and funders. Youth work does not yet have a code of ethics. If it did, then a clause such as that included in the British Association of Social Workers' code might give some legitimacy to challenges from youth workers:

> The worker has the right and duty to bring to the attention of those in power, and of the general public, ways in which the activities of government, society or agencies, create or contribute to hardship and suffering or militate against their relief.
>
> (BASW 1996: para. 9)

Conclusion

The issue of control in youth work always has been and will continue to be the source of many ethical debates and practice dilemmas. What we have called 'control in practice' is essential for all good educational work – involving workers in careful planning of the learning process as they tread a line between the extremes of authoritarian and permissive methods of working – balancing the controlling curriculum with the casual conversation. It is an issue that needs much further exploration and discussion as it is at the heart of youth work practice.

On the other hand, the lengthy arguments of academics about the dangers of practice for control may seem irrelevant, or a luxury, to practitioners working with young people on the streets, searching for the next source of funding or fighting against the closure of a project. We are not suggesting that workers deny the impact of their work on crime reduction, drug abuse or unemployment. Control and management of dangerous and threatening youth has always underpinned much youth work. First, this is because funders frequently require it to do so. Welfare agencies such as health authorities, housing associations or social services expect their investment to produce a reduction in the future demand for their services and changes in behaviour. Whilst local authorities and community groups generally expect to see the efforts of youth workers translated into a lower rates of offending and fewer 'kids on the streets' and 'hanging around'. Second, the public also often expect it to address problems such as 'delinquency' and 'young people making a nuisance of themselves'.

Workers can feel vulnerable to such demands because they are aware that the public and other welfare workers habitually misunderstand their role, perceiving them as leisure workers who, in the words of one teacher, are running 'about playing with bairns all day, and getting paid for it' (Moir 1997: 5). Inevitably workers may fall in line pleading for funds and support on the grounds that they reduce offending and raise the behavioural norms of young people, claiming, as in this example, that closure of a project will be

> devastating on the many underprivileged families and children in the area, who would miss the stimulation of the activities the project provides...that delinquency, vandalism and anti-social behaviour would rise, and that the community could become disheartened and disenchanted once more.
>
> (Ellison 1997: 63)

Yet although such outputs may well flow from youth work intervention, it is hard to prove it.

Implicit within the activity of youth work is a normative belief that it will confer benefits on those who come into contact with the worker; that it will make them better rather than worse people, more educated and more socially responsible, rather than less. It is assumed that youth work will help make them better citizens – individuals who would be more likely to respect the law and behave in morally acceptable ways. All worthwhile education must, in the final analysis, be an act of faith. The alternative is to teach only what can be measured and enumerated.

If youth work is, as we believe, an educational activity then we must learn to trust practitioners and participants mutually to create worthwhile experiences. Funders, managers and the rest of us must resist the temptation to impose a control agenda upon them. We must allow youth workers the freedom to initiate young people into modes of thought, activities, disciplines they would otherwise be denied or would find it difficult to assimilate or engage in unaided. Decisions regarding what are and are not worthwhile modes of thought and activities must be left to practitioners, although they are clearly obligated to engage in dialogue with young people, parents, funders and the wider community if they are to make informed choices. Youth work, as Peters (1959: 97) explains, is essentially a process which seeks to introduce people 'to what is valuable in an intelligible and voluntary manner'. It is the educational purpose which delineates youth work from the mere provision of leisure activities. It also draws a sharp line between youth work and interventions designed to control, manage and contain young people. Consequently, work with young people which sets out specifically to tackle offending and delinquency, to control rather than to educate, swiftly ceases to be youth work.

Bibliography

Baden-Powell, R. (1908) *Scouting For Boys,* London: Arthur Pearson.

Banks, S. (1997) 'The dilemmas of intervention' in J. Roche and S. Tucker (eds) *Youth in Society*, London: Sage/Open University Press.

Bickerdike, K. C. (1926) *The Church and the Boy Outside*, London: Wells Gardner, Darton.

British Association of Social Workers (1996) *A Code of Ethics for Social Work*, Birmingham: BASW.

Collingwood, J. and Collingwood, M. (1990) *Hannah More*, Oxford: Lion Publishing.

Davin, A. (1996) *Growing Up Poor: Home, School and Street in London 1870–1914*, London: Rivers of Oram Press.

Downie, R. and Telfer, E. (1969) *Respect for Persons*, London: Routledge and Kegan Paul.

—— (1980) *Caring and Curing*, London: Methuen.

Ellison, G. (1997) *Twenty Years of Community Development in the East End of Sunderland 1974–1994*, Durham University, unpublished MA dissertation.

France, A. and Wiles, P. (1996) *The Youth Action Scheme: A Report of the National Evaluation*, London: Department for Education and Employment.

—— (1997) 'The Youth Action Scheme and the Future of Youth Work', *Youth and Policy* 57: 1–16.

Freire, P. (1997) *Pedagogy of Hope: Reliving Pedagogy of the Oppressed*, New York: Continuum.

Gate, E. M. (1933) *Roland Philipps: Boy Scout*, London: Roland House.

Haynes, F. (1998) *The Ethical School*, London: Routledge.

Hurt, J. S. (1979) *Elementary Schooling and the Working Classes 1860–1918*, London: RKP.

Jeffs, T. (1997a) 'Changing their ways: youth work and the "underclass theory"' in R. MacDonald (ed.) *Youth, the Underclass and Social Exclusion*, London: Routledge.

—— (1997b) 'Wild things? Young people our new enemy within', *Concept* 8(1): 4–8.

Jeffs, T. and Smith, M. K. (1994) 'Young people, youth work and a new authoritarianism', *Youth and Policy* 46: 17–32.

—— (1996a) '"Getting the dirtbags off the streets": curfews and other solutions to juvenile crime', *Youth and Policy* 53: 1–14.

—— (1996b) *Informal Education*, Ticknall, Derbys: Education Now Books.

Jephcott, P. (1942) *Girls Growing Up*, London: Faber and Faber.

Kant, I. (1964) *Groundwork of the Metaphysics of Morals*, New York: Harper and Row.

Kingman, J. M. and Sidman, E. (1935) *A Manual of Settlement Boys' Work*, Boston: National Federation of Settlements.

Lewin, K., Lippitt, R. and White, R. (1939) 'Patterns of aggressive behaviour in experimentally created social climates' *Journal of Social Psychology* 10: 347–57.

Moir, S, (1997) 'Theory and practice: towards a critical pedagogy of youth work', *Concept* 7(1) 5–7.

Oakeshott, M. (1962) *Rationalism in Politics*, New York: Basic Books.

Peters, R. S. (1959) *Authority, Responsibility and Education*, London: Unwin.

—— (1963) *Education as Initiation*, London: Evans Brothers.

Russell, B. (1932) *Education and the Social Order*, London: Unwin.

Russell, C. and Russell, L. (1932) *Lads' Clubs: Their History, Organisation and Management*, London: A. C. Black.

Secretan, R. (1931) *London Below Bridges*, London: Godfrey Bles.

Shotton, J. (1993) *No Master High or Low: Libertarian Education and Schooling 1890–1990*, Bristol: Libertarian Education.

Smith, M. (1994) *Local Education. Community, Conversation, Praxis*, Milton Keynes: Open University Press.

Smith, D. and Paylor, I. (1997) 'Reluctant heroes: youth workers and crime prevention', *Youth and Policy* 57: 17–28.

7

THE YOUTH WORKER AS CONVERTER

Ethical issues in religious youth work

Maxine Green

Introduction

The youth worker as converter is a very powerful concept. It invokes a whole range of assumptions about the role of youth workers and the outcomes of the youth work they undertake. It is an ethical minefield. However, it is essential that this somewhat controversial area of work is openly discussed and debated at this time when statutory youth provision is being reduced and there is an increase in the work of the voluntary sector. Many of these new youth workers are being appointed by religious organisations.

The debate about the youth worker as converter has a number of features. First, it draws on the history of work with young people. On the negative side there has been work which has corrupted the essential principles of youth work by coercing young people to join particular religious movements. On the positive side, there is an acceptance that religions and political movements have been quintessential in the formation of the youth service. Second, the debate is set in the context of a society where adult members of religious organisations are keen to 'pass on' to the younger generation what they see as core values and practices. There are real concerns voiced by older religious people that religious truths may be 'lost' both to the young people and to society as a whole. However, at the same time this urgency may lead to poor practice where a desire to 'convert' results in the exploitation of the religious vulnerability of young people. Finally, it is a debate that is focused on ideas and concepts and how these are interpreted. 'Conversion' is a form of change and it is undeniable that change is expected in youth work.

110

The questions are what sort of change and conversion is appropriate, and what is the role of the youth worker as a professional in that change?

This chapter aims to explore some of the background against which these assumptions are made. It will explore the ethical issues, both for religious youth work and for the professional youth worker. The discussion focuses largely on the Christian religion and draws particularly on the experience of the Church of England. The chapter demonstrates that ideologically inspired youth work is a complex issue and careful thought is needed to avoid the 'knee-jerk' reaction that often accompanies this debate. The intention is not to devise a code of practice for religious or political youth work (Banks 1996), but to raise the ethical issues that surround such work. To improve good practice of work that is based both within religious organisations and secular youth work it is important that a rigorous and challenging dialogue is encouraged.

Background

There is no one model of 'religious youth work'. Different major faiths and denominations use different methods to achieve different aims and this work has varied over time and ranges from best practice to very poor practice. There is no doubt that at the 'poor practice' end of the spectrum there has been considerable abuse of young people where powerful concepts of salvation and the afterlife have been used to instil regimented, unthinking following. In social science, Freud (1927) saw religion as a means of controlling the masses who were unable to internalise the concept of self-realisation, and Marx (1938) saw it as 'the opium of the people' which mystified citizens into accepting subjugation. Work with people that draws on ideological and religious frameworks is exceptionally powerful and as such is open to abuse, as well as use.

In a more positive frame, religious thinking has inspired and campaigned for huge changes in social reform, welfare and education, and Christians and Christian organisations were at the forefront of the foundation of the youth service and subsequent developments:

> The 'youth service' in England developed in the late nineteenth century. The earliest voluntary youth organisations were started by philanthropic individuals, many of whom were Christian. The Young Men's Christian Association (YMCA) and the Girls' Friendly Society are amongst those

that aimed to provide education and leisure opportunities for young workers. In the second half of the century charity work on behalf of working young people mushroomed and was led by city centre evangelical missions and ragged schools where clubs for young people began to be formed. In 1884 there were 300 institutes and working boys clubs in the Diocese of London alone and most of these were associated with churches.

(Church of England 1996: 148)

It is important to note that the Church of England, at local, regional and national level, has played a significant role in supporting, contributing to and, in many instances, pioneering a wide range of youth work initiatives. Notable among these pioneering aspects which influenced subsequent statutory provision have been the numerous city centre-based detached youth projects; night shelters for the young; hostel accommodation schemes for unmarried young mothers; motor car and bike projects and innovative schemes of training for part-time youth workers.

(ibid.: 150)

These extracts show that the church has had great influence on the youth service in the past. This influence continues in the present both through existing structures and with the rapid increase in the number of churches that are employing full-time and part-time youth workers. It is difficult to obtain precise figures which document this rise nationally, but individual Church of England dioceses report the number of full-time youth workers employed trebling or quadrupling between 1993 and 1997 (personal communication), and this is accompanied by a corresponding increase in sessional workers employed. This pattern is mirrored in other denominations, with a significant number of workers employed on an ecumenical basis.

There are several reasons behind this shift to employing more youth workers in the church. These include the church being concerned about the number of young people joining as full members and wanting to ensure that the faith is passed on to the younger generation. There is an awareness of the 'spiritual rights' of young people and a desire to empower them by giving them access to their spiritual heritage. This investment in the future also extends to wanting the best for society and ensuring that the religious perspective is not lost. There is also a desire for the institution of the church to continue and an understanding that this demands new members. Many churches have focused on young people as they recognise adolescence as being a critical period for faith development and they plan their work programme to reflect this.

There has been a large drop in the number of young people who consider themselves full members of the church. *Youth A Part* (Church of England 1996: 13) includes information on young people at Sunday Services in the Church of England and records a drop of 35 per cent in attendance among 14–17 year olds between 1987 and 1994 and a corresponding drop of 34 per cent among those aged 18–21 years. Similar patterns of decreasing attendance are found within the other major denominations, and this picture is matched in membership of young people in political parties and other institutions such as the Scouts and Guides. This fall in membership at one level puts pressure on the institution to maintain itself, but what is more important for many people who are part of the organisation is that young people should have access to the ideology and to important truths known to the organisation.

Educating the 'next generation' is part of the responsibility of a society and it is essential that skills, knowledge and values be passed on to young people to equip the community as a whole. It is particularly important for religious movements to be able to offer their history and practice to young people. Failure to pass on these ideas not only injures the organisations, but also disempowers young people who are then unable to build on previous work. Western societies accept the responsibility to 'educate' young people by providing opportunities for them to become literate, numerate and gain an understanding of the world. There is also a commitment by society to spiritual development. This has been referred to in government youth work reports published since 1944. Lord Redcliffe-Maud defined the aim of youth services as:

> To offer individual young people in their leisure time, opportunities to discover and develop their personal resources of body, mind and spirit and thus equip themselves to live the life of mature, creative and responsible members of a free society.
>
> (HMSO 1969: 55)

The rights of young people for religious education accompany the responsibility of organisations to offer their thinking and practice to the 'next generation'. This does not mean that young people should be 'trained', inducted or programmed, but that they have a chance to become familiar with different life frameworks. The preciousness of these life frameworks is not generally accepted in the 'over-developed' world, in contrast to some older societies – for example, the Seneca of North America (Wallace 1972), where receiving knowledge of myth and ritual is seen as a privilege.

The report *How Faith Grows* (Church of England 1991) describes different theories of faith development and 'stages' which people pass through as they acquire a faith. 'Stage three' details a wish to belong to a faith crowd or current, where many people join together in sharing belief and practice. This stage occurs commonly at the time of adolescence when existentialist questions are asked along with a search for a future adult identity. Young people are particularly vulnerable at this time to groups who give them a sense of belonging and being loved. In the worst cases, this need is exploited unscrupulously and powerful techniques such as 'love bombing' are used to recruit young people to cults and new religious movements (Barker 1992). The need to belong to something bigger and meaningful has been behind many political movements and can be abused – as, for example, the Hitler Youth.

Young people have a right to have the theological and political tools to enable them to make choices about different groups. Experiences of responsible organisations can give them balanced life frameworks by which they can assess new groups they may encounter so that they may approach these groups with reason and caution. It is important where there is a will to pass on skills, beliefs and experience that this is done in a way which is empowering for young people. There is a real difference between good youth work which gives young people increased opportunities, and indoctrination and coercion (Green 1997). It is especially important for religious organisations that have centuries of experience of 'conversion' not to abuse this knowledge as they offer opportunities of spiritual and political development to young people. This is even more pertinent where falling numbers may endanger the life of the institution itself and the need for members becomes a primary aim.

The ethics of youth work in religious organisations

The youth worker is often the catalyst between the traditional society and young people. By working alongside young people the youth worker can enable political, social or religious debate and thus offer a forum in which this development can take place. This is an essential role, both for the society and the rights of young people.

The ethical issues that surround youth work relate to how this process occurs. Clarity is needed about what sort of ideological youth work constitutes good practice and whether there is some work undertaken with young people that is unethical. The first issue is to establish what is 'good youth work'. Banks (1996) says that, in the absence of many of the 'traits' of a profession, youth work has established a collective identity somewhat patchily and argues for increased opportunities to debate professional values and practice. Debate and discussion took place at the ministerial conferences in the 1980s and 1990s. From these emerged an agreed National Statement of Purpose for Youth Work that provides a value base for the profession:

> The purpose of youth work is to redress all forms of inequality and to ensure equality of opportunity for all young people to fulfil their potential as empowered individuals and young people of group and communities and to support young people during transition to adulthood.
>
> (National Youth Agency 1993: 42)

Informal education, empowerment, equal opportunities and participation were agreed as the basic professional principles. Although there must be discussion as to how these terms are used, they do provide useful starting points to debate whether work with young people conforms to good professional practice. For example, education, particularly informal education, is the principal process in youth work. This can be used as a starting point to assess a piece of practice. Using a case example from a hypothetical church project, I will now illustrate how a situation may be approached in three different ways: using an informal education approach; a directive approach; and a conversion approach.

The situation involves a young woman, Teri, coming to a youth worker, Jim, wanting help. She explains that she is depressed, she is having problems with a relationship and with her parents.

1   If an informal education model is used, Jim, the youth worker, will help Teri to explore and analyse the situation. This will be by using open questions that will enable Teri to think of all the aspects relating to her circumstances. Jim will encourage this divergent exploration and the ownership of the problem will

remain with Teri. After, Jim will help Teri to sum up the range of options open to her and will help her to explore the 'pros and cons' of each option. Teri being encouraged to reject the least suitable options and decide on a course of action follows this. Jim can then help Teri to identify the resources she needs to enable that change. Teri can then go and do what she has decided. Another way the youth worker can be helpful to her is by being there to debrief the course of action and to enable Teri to analyse the situation for future developments.

2   A more directive approach may occur when a worker has a strong single framework that he uses in all situations. In this case, when Teri approaches Jim he is already making decisions about Teri in relation to his own framework, considering for example: 'Is she a Christian?', 'Is she saved?'. The worker will then hear the situation within this framework. Although the worker may listen well to Teri, there may be a script at the back of his mind which impairs the informal education process. Thus, Teri's 'problem' may be seen in terms of the faith of the worker, and tenets of faith may be used to solve the problem rather than enable Teri to address the problem as she sees it. The process is much more likely to be like a consultation where Teri lays out the situation, the worker ponders and comes up with a solution that is 'sold' to Teri and then takes some responsibility in enabling this solution to happen. Jim may continue to work to reinforce and support Teri encouraging her to adopt his own ideological framework.

3   A still more limiting approach is where a single solution is seen as the answer to all Teri's problems. Here the worker may entreat Teri to 'take Jesus as her personal saviour' and convince her that all will be well after making such a decision.

In the first example of informal education above, the power is left with the young person and the youth worker takes the facilitating role. A good youth worker will be able to help the young person to come up with a divergent range of possible outcomes which may meet the young person's enquiry or need. Although the youth worker will have his or her own values and experience, the most important aspect of this work is that the young person is given space to explore options, supported while she makes choices and empowered to develop through the experience.

In the second example, the worker's own values have framed the encounter. The worker has allowed his own values to frame the problem and decrease the range of options that Teri has available to her. The exploratory nature of the process is impaired and the worker disempowers Teri by taking her problem away and 'solving it' and thus not allowing Teri to develop and grow from the experience.

In the third scenario, the needs of the worker to convert Teri are so strong that the whole informal education process is by-passed and, instead of enabling Teri to address the problems that she faces, the agenda becomes that of the worker. Teri is not empowered, is not able to use her situation to develop, therefore this is not informal education and not youth work.

Where there is an aim to convert or evangelise, there is tremendous pressure not to take the 'risk' of exploring a divergent range of choices with the young person but to present a single viewpoint or solution. This is even stronger when the faith of the youth workers is very powerful in their own lives and may have led them to a vivid and personal transformation which they want to share. This may mean that the work is based on a behavioural model with the young people being rewarded for making certain choices and electing to adopt the values of the institution. These rewards can be linked to a sense of belonging and worth, which is a strong motivator for young people as they move towards an adult identity. Although the short-term effects of this sort of work can be dramatic, it is questionable what sort of attitude change there is in the long term. Many dynamic evangelistic events, following a 'Billy Graham approach' or using multimedia rock concert techniques, produce dramatic conversions that may be short lived compared to a more reasoned faith acquired through a more open informal education process. There is a question concerning the efficacy of behavioural models of conversion. However, it is still the case that whatever the motives, youth work must be participative and empowering. 'Solving the problem' for a young person by offering a single religious or political solution, or the conditional offer of belonging in exchange for membership, is not informal education and is not youth work.

Although a committed or visionary youth worker has a more overt belief system, no youth workers are ideologically blank and devoid of personal values, and these will undoubtedly inform their work. All youth workers should consider how their personal values impinge on the work and what is professionally valid. It is especially important for religious youth workers to examine their practice if they work for institutions where there is pressure on them to gain new members or 'deepen' beliefs of young people. The ethical issues which are most pertinent relate to the role of the worker, the process of youth work and the desired outcomes of the work.

The role of youth worker is crucial in the ethical debate. The informal education process provides space for the young person to explore personal and social issues for their own development. It is important that this working space is held by the youth worker and is not crowded out by the worker's own beliefs or values. If an informal education process is adopted, it is appropriate for youth workers to share their own faith when asked provided the workers make it clear that the belief is held personally and is one of many options which is available to the young people. The youth worker as the facilitator of the process works with the young person to explore the issues and options in the widest sense and, if the young person wishes, helps to make choices and support change. As the youth worker may be a role model to the young person, it is important that the worker explores fairly the range of options available and speaks of his or her own belief choices frankly and openly but without 'closing down' other possibilities for the young person.

The process of youth work is not the same as the content of the work and, although the process should meet the criteria of 'education, empowerment, equality of opportunity and participation', work can be explicitly religious and still be good youth work. For example, a piece of work may involve young people conducting worship in a church. If the young people are aware and have 'opted in', and if they are involved and not coerced or manipulated, then this will enable them to develop and they will be empowered and educated through the process. Although the content of the work is explicitly religious, the process is informal education and the result can be good quality youth work. The main ethical issue rests on the awareness of young people within the process and whether they are enabled or disabled in making choices.

The desired outcomes, or aims or objectives, can also indicate whether youth work is in accord with the principles of 'education, empowerment, equality of opportunity and participation'. If the principal aim of the work with young people is to make new or better members of a religious organisation, then the informal education process will inevitably be contorted. No longer is the work functioning on the agenda of the young people in negotiation with the youth worker, but the worker is working to a specific outcome which is predetermined and thus the young person will be more likely to be moulded and directed to meet the aim. The pressure will be less empowering and more directive and will diverge from the informal education model of making informed choices as described above.

> A religion can only encourage the personal freedom of its young people towards their future if the religion is free with regard to its own future. If Christian faith sought merely to reduplicate itself, to form young Christians who were the exact repetition of the previous generation, to pass on Christian faith as if it were a parcel handed down from generation to generation, then it would be very difficult to distinguish between the passing on of this sort of thing and closed authoritative instruction or even indoctrination.
>
> (British Council of Churches 1976: 23)

Religious institutions do not necessarily have narrow or convergent objectives. There is a desire for political and religious awareness and competence in many institutions that can be a primary aim, with a secondary wish that a proportion of young people might choose to affiliate with a particular ideology or institution.

> What we pass onto our children is not the painting but the paint box.
>
> (ibid.: 24)

> If we conceive of the locale of religious education as a dynamic, flexible, and forward looking community of learners and teachers, what kinds of goals do we seek? Rather than outline specific goals in terms of description, what we need are areas in which generalised goals may be established. If we take a pluralistic and flexible view of the meaning of religious maturity, we cannot expect results in terms of fixed beliefs or codes of behaviour. If we take seriously the meaning of human freedom responding to vague stimuli, both human and divine, we may hope to evoke insights but we cannot determine assembly line results.
>
> (Miller 1990: 258)

Institutions operating more open policies will aim for an ideological maturity amongst the young people worked with. If the institutions also offer real participation, empowerment and equality in their youth work this can represent best practice in the field. An example follows relating to the 'Time for God' scheme:

Every year about 140 young people give up to a year of their time to the Time for God scheme. They are placed in churches, projects, and other Christian organisations and receive their board and keep and a little spending money... The volunteers are trained, supported and carefully matched so that their skills can benefit the placement and they can learn and develop through the work.

(Church of England 1996: 78)

Another element that plays a seminal role in the collective under-standing of professional ethics is the training and qualification of youth workers. The standards that lay down the level of training and attainment that is sufficient to become a 'qualified youth worker' has largely been determined by the Joint Negotiating Committee and the National Youth Agency in its role of endorsing courses. Although many youth work courses have been run by colleges which were founded by religious denominations, the courses that have been professionally endorsed have largely been secular, with the religious element implicit and integral rather than explicitly explored. There have been recent moves to establish 'youth ministry' courses that are more overtly evangelical, and where theological training runs parallel to youth work theory and practice. The ethical issue that is raised by such courses is whether the principles of informal education are integral to the work, and whether the course encourages participation and empowerment of young people whilst promoting equality of opportunity.

Religious work that uses a more directive behavioural style may be using a more formal education model that can be effective and useful to the young people but differs from youth work. The differ-ences occur in that the focus may be on the desired outcomes (bringing to faith or deepening faith) and that the agenda is set by the organisation. Although it can be argued that young people can be empowered by the outcomes of such training, they are not neces-sarily empowered by the process. A parallel can be made with statutory education where young people are undoubtedly empow-ered by gaining academic qualifications, but do not actively participate in setting the agenda or negotiating the process.

Ethical issues for youth workers

There are ethical issues that youth workers encounter personally when being employed by an organisation which is in existence because of the belief system it expounds. There are questions about the extent to which the youth worker's personal faith corresponds to that of the organisation and how where there are differences the situation is resolved.

Many working in religious youth work are drawn in with a strong sense of vocation and with strong ideological aims. The worker may have a powerful personal need to 'share the story' and this may impair the central experiential element of informal education through youth work. It may be that such a worker would be more comfortable with a delivered formal education approach and much religious instruction is delivered using more directive practice. In some faiths this is part of a process of traditional dissemination and there is an understanding of the strengths and weaknesses of this sort of delivery. Nesbitt and Jackson's (1994) work with Hindu and Sikh children shows a range of formal and informal methods employed (Nesbitt 1993). It is important for there to be clarity about what process is being used and that a more directive training approach is not seen as youth work. The strength of the youth work process in spiritual development is important, and open, participative ways of working are to be encouraged. When youth work is being established, questions that may be asked include:

- Are the aims and objectives narrow and predefined and do they relate to specific desired changes in the young people?
- Are young people empowered through this project and are they actively involved in shaping it?
- Is there equality of opportunity in the project?
- Does the project use the informal education process?

As a group of practitioners with a commitment and investment in youth work as a 'profession', it is entirely appropriate and responsible for us to ask these questions of each other's practice, both formally and informally, regardless of faith or ideological position.

For those youth workers who wish to use professional youth-work methods, there may be difficulty where individual young people make choices which conflict with personally held values. An example may be a young person choosing to have an abortion where the youth worker's principles are against this. It is important in this situation that if the youth worker cannot enable the young person to explore a range of choices then they have to make this clear and allow the young person decide whether the worker is the most appropriate person to help. What matters most is that there is an integrity in the relationship and just as doctors may declare a personal position that alters the consultation, so may the youth worker make a similar declaration. Other youth workers may put increased value on the youth work process rather than the outcome and are able suspend their own judgement and preference allowing the young person to make an informed choice. In this situation it is important for the youth worker to realise the impossibility of being 'totally objective' but to endeavour to be aware of the impact of their own value system on the process.

Another key area for the youth worker to address is their awareness of the vulnerability of young people as they search for meaning, identity and a sense of belonging. This is especially important for those youth workers whose values reflect such concepts as salvation, damnation, redemption or reincarnation. These concepts are very powerful and have to be used sensitively so that young people retain control and power over their own lives.

Conclusion

It is very easy to point a finger from a secular youth work position at religious or political institutions and be convinced of poor or partial practice. It is important to note, though, that the youth service was born out of the conscience of individual Christians and religious groups and much of the emphasis within youth work of social justice has its roots in Victorian Christian campaigning and service.

All youth workers have a value system that informs their work, and effective dialogue between youth work practitioners of all ideological, religious or political persuasions can only be beneficial in the development of 'professional' ethics. It is apparent that the discussion of ethics and youth work needs to be a more collective exercise to sharpen the focus and confidence of youth work practitioners. There are several principles that are central to any ethical debate on work with young people from a particular ideological perspective, be that religious, political or single-issue groups. These are as follows:

- It is ethically sound for organisations to share their perspectives, skills, knowledge and values. It is not only sound but it is irresponsible of organisations to withhold collective knowledge and traditions that belong to everyone in society regardless of age.

- Young people have a right to develop spiritually and politically as well as mentally, physically and socially. It is not enough to leave this development to haphazard processes, but there should be an understanding of the process of how people develop frameworks of thought and living and this should be part of the youth work curriculum. Secular youth work should examine the degree that religious and political development of young people is addressed in the curriculum and make appropriate provision for this.
- Youth work is a means to empower young people politically and religiously. By having an understanding of established ideological frameworks young people are able to use these and be enabled by them, and are also able to be critically reflective of groups abusing the youth work process for institutional gain.
- Qualified youth work practitioners should feel confident to challenge ideologically based youth work using the National Statement of Purpose and other sets of ethical principles developed collectively through training and debate.
- Through this increased confidence in practice youth workers should feel able to challenge and resist unprofessional work that disempowers young people, especially that work which exploits the adolescent search for identity, belonging and meaning.
- Religious organisations should be encouraged to examine their work with young people and use best professional practice. This would enable their youth workers to work with young people to facilitate growth and development while offering information about the organisation.

Active dialogue between youth workers with the whole range of ideological, political and religious viewpoints can only challenge and sharpen the professional edge and ethics of youth work.

Bibliography

Banks, S. (1996) 'Youth work, informal education and professionalisation: the issues in the 1990s', *Youth and Policy* 54: 13–25.

Barker, E. (1992) *New Religious Movements*, London: HMSO.

British Council of Churches (1976) *Child and the Church*, London: CGMC.

Church of England (1991) *How Faith Grows*, London: National Society/Church Housing Publishing.

—— (1996) *Youth A Part*, London: Church House Publishing.

Freud, S. (1927) *Future of an Illusion*, London: Penguin.

Green, M. J. (1997) 'A religious perspective for youth work' in N. Kendra and I. Ledgerwood (eds) *The Challenge for the Future: Towards the New Millennium for the Youth Service*, Lyme Regis: Russell House.

HMSO (1969) *Youth and Community Work in the 70s*, London: HMSO.

Keesing, R. (1969) *Cultural Anthropology*, Orlando: Holt, Rinehart and Winston.

Marx, K. (1938) *Capital*, London: George Allen and Unwin.

Miller, R. C. (1990) 'Theology and the future of religious education' in L. Francis and A. Thatcher (eds) *Christian Perspectives for Education*, Leominster: Gracewing.

National Youth Agency (1993) *Report of the Third Ministerial Conference*, Leicester: NYA.

Nesbitt, E. (1993) 'The transmission of Christian tradition in an ethically diverse society', in R. Barot (ed.) *Religion and Ethnicity: Minorities and Social Change in the Metropolis*, Kampen, Netherlands: Kok Pharos.

Nesbitt, E. and Jackson, R. (1994) 'Aspects of cultural transmission in a diaspora Sikh community', *Journal of Sikh Studies* 18(1): 55–67.

Wallace, A. (1972) *The Death and Rebirth of the Seneca*, New York, USA: Vintage.

8

YOUTH WORKERS AS MEDIATORS AND INTERPRETERS

Ethical issues in work with black young people

Umme F. Imam

Introduction

This chapter explores some of the complexities which arise in working with black young people growing up within multi-ethnic social frameworks. All youth workers mediate and negotiate within and between structures and authorities as they support individuals and groups of young people. However, those working with black young people work between distinctive and unequal cultural systems with different, and sometimes conflicting, ethics and values drawn from opposing philosophical traditions. Some of the tensions that arise are explored within the context of racism, the supremacy of Western values and the principles underpinning youth work in Britain.

The analysis is undertaken at two levels. The first section addresses issues relevant to all black communities in Britain, focusing on the primacy of Western values and ethical traditions and the implications this has had for work with young people from minority cultures and communities. In the second section, with the help of examples from practice, ways in which youth workers have mediated between different value systems and challenged ethnocentric values, both in dominant and within minority communities are examined. This is done with specific reference to work with young people of South Asian descent. The aim is to highlight the distinctive issues faced by workers and their contribution to practitioner ethics in the field of youth work. In illustrating particular issues faced by youth workers in both black-led and mainstream statutory and voluntary agencies, examples are drawn from interviews and discussions with workers and young people.

Terminology

In recent years usage of the term 'black' as a political term referring to people who share the common experience of racism in Britain has been contested on the grounds that it is essentialist and denies ethnicity and cultural identity (Brah 1992: 127–31; Hall 1992; Anthias and Yuval Davies 1992). It is argued that developments in black cultural politics have resulted in a shift in the identity politics of black communities in Britain, and that a new phase has emerged which demands a deeper analysis which addresses ethnicity and diversity and the disaggregation of the different constituencies that came together under the term 'black' (Hall 1992). In youth work practice, in the absence of a more acceptable term, practitioners and young people continue to identify closely with the term and, as Bandana Ahmad asserts, the term 'black' is not used to deny cultural diversity and difference but continues to be 'a source of unified strength and solidarity opening up more opportunities for celebrating and affirming ethnic identity' (1990: 2–3).

The term 'South Asian' is used to refer to people of Bangladeshi, Indian and Pakistani heritage who share common origins in the Indian sub-continent, a heritage of collectivist cultures and the experience of 'cultural racism' in Britain (Ahmed 1986). The communities, homogenised by the term 'Asian' in common usage, include a heterogeneous group of people who are differentiated on the basis of gender relations, language, religion, social traditions, social class or caste, rural/urban origins and different trajectories of migration. Change and modification is ongoing in response to the economic and political context, and contact with white and other black communities is producing an ever-widening range of diasporic cultures. The term 'Western' is used to refer to the economically and politically powerful nations and societies, primarily in Western Europe and North America. 'Non-Western' is used here to refer to the developing nations and societies in Africa and Asia.

I interpret 'values' as stable and enduring beliefs which serve as standards and guide selection and evaluation of behaviour, people and events (Smith and Schwartz 1997). They are relative to one another in importance and an ordered set of values forms a system of value priorities. Cultures and individuals can be characterised by their systems of value priorities; these are the central and distinguishing features of individuals and cultures. 'Ethics' are norms of behaviour people follow concerning what is right and wrong, good or bad and are inevitably influenced by the values that are prioritised at the individual or cultural level. The term 'culture' may be defined as an organised system of shared meanings which members of that culture attribute to persons and objects which make up their culture (Smith and Bond 1993). The values that are prioritised in a culture influence the norms and ethics that are salient in that culture.

Youth work in a plural society

Two important factors complicate the work of those involved with black young people as they move between and negotiate different cultural contexts. The first is the dominance of the majority culture, ethics and values and the marginalisation of minority cultures in the wider society. Second, complexities arise through the interface of individualist cultures of the normative majority and the collectivist cultures of the subordinate minorities.

The hegemony of dominant values

Youth work does not take place in a vacuum nor do youth workers hold neutral principles and values. Both are subject to cultural and societal influences which impact upon the work and workers. In a culturally diverse society it is expected that there should be a heterogeneity of cultures, traditions, ethics and values, which are fluid and dynamic and interact and intersect to form new configurations and positions (Woolett *et al.* 1994). Maclaren explains why, despite pluralism in society, the superiority of the majority values prevails:

> with diversity comes a 'transparent norm' constructed and administered by the 'host society' that creates a false consensus. This is because the normative grid that locates cultural diversity at the same time serves to contain cultural difference: 'the universalism that paradoxically permits diversity masks ethnocentric norms'.
>
> (Maclaren 1995: 213–14)

In Britain, there has been active resistance to the acceptance that Britain is a pluralist society. Despite the acknowledgement of the multi-ethnic nature of Britain by the New Right (Gordon and Klug 1986) there has been a concerted effort to establish

> the primacy of an imagined 'British' culture, which renders the cultures, and hence values of ethnic minority communities marginal and subordinate to the political project that is the British Nation.
>
> (Husband 1995: 86)

Consequently, in their work with black young people, workers find themselves negotiating a two-tier value system. The differential occurs because, despite the pluralism in British society, the values of the majority are presented as universal and progressive and those of minorities inferior and regressive. The inequality is further confirmed by assumptions that minority cultures are fixed and static and their movement from one ethnic context to another has involved a single cultural change through adaptation to the new situation and in relation to the majority, rather than the fluid and continuous change attributed to majority cultures (Woolett *et al.* 1994). Also inherent is the inference that there is a dualism between being Western and non-Western, which limits the possibilities for complication and dynamism. This dichotomy is too simplistic in view of the changing kaleidoscopic nature of ethnic identities and the complexities which arise out of the interface between different cultural systems and intersections with gender, social class or caste, urban and rural origins, disability and sexual orientation. Amina Mama asserts that:

> multiplicity rather than duality characterises metropolitan life, and that people inhabit not one but several contexts simultaneously, so that this has become a normal state of affairs in a post colonial world. This is a world in which no context is as fixed or as static as assumed by the manichean and dualistic colonial frameworks that counterpoise West and non-West. Instead cultural and social conditions are undergoing constant change and exchange.
>
> (Mama 1995:13)

Work with young black people needs to be focused on helping them to cope with the demands of the multiple cultural systems they inhabit. The situation would be complex in itself without the addition of racism and cultural oppression to the dynamics, and their influence on individuals and how they conceive of themselves.

The worker's role is to support the self-emancipation of young people through promoting understanding of how the ideologies and values of the majority influence and limit their lives, inhibiting participation and equality (Smith 1988). Practitioners need to evaluate and assess the extent to which young people understand and/or internalise dominant values. It is important to consider whether values expressed by young people are reflective of conscious individual choice as opposed to their response to racism.

Opposing value systems: individualism versus collectivism

Mark Smith (1988: 99), commenting on the ethnocentrism in youth work, points out that the 'concept of self that informs much discussion about social education is distinctly Western and individualistic'. An indiscriminate application of Western concepts without considering their relevance to people who may not share, or partly share, these modes of thinking reflects inequality in practice. Therefore, in working with black young people who are also part of non-Western and collectivist cultures, an understanding of the values prioritised by them is essential for effective practice.

In the last decade considerable attention has been devoted to the paradigm of individualism–collectivism in cross-cultural psychology in the search for universals for human values and social behaviour. Attention has been given to identifying and analysing this at both individual and cultural levels. On the cultural level, the distinguishing feature is the priority given to personal interests or to group interests: the tendency to value independence, emotional detachment, personal achievement and competition or to value interdependence, emotional closeness, group achievement and cooperation (Triandis 1995, cited in Smith and Schwartz 1997). Black young people are socialised into families that are part of collectivist cultures and which value interdependence and cooperation. They are simultaneously socialised into the individualistic culture of the majority through their peers, schools and other institutions. They may therefore adopt a combination of values and reflect this in the way they conceive of themselves. As black young people and black workers are socialised simultaneously into both majority and minority cultures this gives them what Narayan (1989) terms 'epistemic advantage' over their white counterparts in that they can occupy more than one context simultaneously. She explains that this advantage is a consequence of the historical inequality which imposed a Western worldview on non-Western people, while the converse has not happened.

Individualism and collectivism have been defined as distinguishing features of Western and non-Western cultures respectively (Marsella *et al.* 1985). The significant difference between these two constructs is in conceiving self as an independent entity motivated by personal standards or as interdependent and part of social groups, motivated by social expectations (Markus and Kitayama 1991). The majority of humankind share aspects of collectivism. The West, where individualism prevails, covers less than 30 per cent of humanity and, even within this, ethnic minorities and lower socio-economic status groups tend to be collectivist (Singelis *et al.* 1995, cited in Kagitcibasi 1997: 5).

Kagitcibasi's (1996) work on the development of a sense of self in different cultural and socio-economic contexts mediated by the family is of particular relevance. She differentiated between the Relational Self and the Separated Self. The Relational Self develops where there is total emotional and material interdependence and intergenerational interdependence is essential for family livelihood. The Separated Self develops where intergenerational interdependence is not needed for family livelihood. She proposes a third category of self, seen specifically in developed urban areas of societies with collectivist cultures, which combines the relational and autonomous orientations: the 'Autonomous-Related Self' which develops where material interdependence in the family weakens but the emotional interdependence continues. This combines both individualistic and collectivist elements and satisfies both the human needs for autonomy and relatedness.

Recent empirical evidence, particularly by non-Western researchers, suggests that these two constructs, individualism and collectivism, are not necessarily polarised and may coexist in individuals and groups – in different situations or with different groups (Mishra 1994; Sinha and Tripathi 1994). Equality in youth work practice can be promoted through understanding of the ways in which individualism and collectivism are interlinked in young people's lives and how they influence both social expectations and behaviour. In relation to the pluralist society in which youth work takes place, therefore, professional ethics should not just draw from Western liberal traditions of individualism which promote the 'ethics of justice'. Further consideration needs to be given to the inclusion of an 'ethics of care' based on interdependence, connectedness, cooperation and collective responsibility (Banks 1995: 34–5), as some feminist theories have also emphasised (Chodorow 1989; Gilligan 1982). This would be in contradiction to the dominant

Western ways of thinking; nevertheless, these need to be interrogated and deconstructed, if necessary, if we are to acknowledge and validate marginalised and subordinated modes of thinking and being (Maclaren 1995).

Ethical issues in working with young people of South Asian heritage

In light of the preceding discussion on the dominance of Western values, we cannot assume a common or neutral ethical framework which may be of relevance to workers working with all constituencies of young people growing up in Britain. Practitioner ethics are socially constructed and reflect dominant norms; social and institutional structures will inevitably define and normalise ethics in any area of work. Banks (1997: 222–3) suggests that the ethical dilemmas commonly encountered in the welfare professions fall into three main categories: conflicts between the self-determination (autonomy) of the service user and what the professional considers to be in their best interests; conflicts between the rights and welfare of different people; and conflicts between personal and professional values/agency values.

The categorisation seems simplistic when applied to work with minority communities that may not share the values arising from Western individualistic thinking. Broadly, practitioners working with black young people face similar dilemmas and, in addition, there are also those which arise due to different and unequal value systems of workers, agencies, communities and young people. In practice, this is significant in two ways. First, there is the assumption of majority values and norms, particularly those relating to individualism. Little attention is given to the complexity of young people's lives and the continuous drawing and redrawing of boundaries as they negotiate different cultural contexts and changing social and cultural landscapes. Second, issues arise due to conflicting values of workers and the agencies and institutions which recruit and employ them. These vary according to values, policies and working practices of employing agencies which may have very different approaches (ranging from liberal to radical) to equal opportunities issues (Jewson and Mason 1992).

Self-determination, rights and culture

Central to youth work practice is the principle of self-determination, the non-directive enabling of young people to make decisions and choices in their lives leading to self-emancipation (Smith 1988). The concept of self-determination has come from rights-based approaches to moral thought which are rooted in Western liberal traditions and philosophies. In particular, the right to self-determination is firmly established in Kantian principles and the recognition that individuals should have autonomy in making their own choices and decisions (Banks 1995). It has been widely interpreted ranging from the absolute right of the individual to do as they please, to intervention by practitioners based on their beliefs about what is in the best interests of the individual. In youth work practice, despite a parentalist approach, the emphasis has been on promoting self-determination through personal and social education. This has reflected the majority individualistic values with little consideration given to the fact that interdependence rather than independence is the cultural particularity for black young people, and freedom of choice is circumscribed by emotional interdependence and responsibility to family and community (Ahmad 1990: 14). Practitioners are faced with difficult choices when self-determination by the young person results in conflict with family expectations and interdependence. Another problem with individualist (Kantian) approaches is that when there is conflict between the rights of two individuals – for example, parent and young person – how do we decide whose right to self-determination should prevail? In the case of conflict between the individual and family, mediation between the two generations involves more than just the issues around age and generation. It also involves work between different configurations of cultural systems – the monocultural perspectives or the 'old ethnicities' of some parents and the 'new ethnicities' of the young people (Hall 1992).

The example below demonstrates this conflict between the rights of two individuals:

> The youth worker in an Asian women's project was approached by a member whose daughter Asha attended the young women's group. The mother was concerned about her daughter's behaviour as she was going out with a white boyfriend and seen to be 'behaving inappropriately' in community settings. This had provoked great censure within the community as she was seen to be too 'Westernised and moving out of her culture'. As a widowed single parent the mother was quite distressed about her daughter's behaviour and the implications this would have for her own honour

and respect, as well as that of her other daughters within the community. She asked the youth worker to use her influence to dissuade the young woman from seeing her white boyfriend. Asha had also discussed the situation with the worker. She seemed to be quite serious about the relationship and felt that she should have the right to make her own decision about her future partner and did not really care what the community thought of her.

In discussing and analysing the situation and her own intervention, the worker said she recognised the pressures on the mother from the local community and empathised with her. She also recognised that the young woman, brought up in Western society, was reflecting the predominant individualistic values. The differences in perspectives were inevitable as they had developed through different social and cultural experiences in the Indian sub-continent and in Britain. Being part of the community, she had a good understanding of the role expectations and responsibilities of each of the individuals concerned. Her own experience of growing up and living in two different value systems informed her understanding of the dynamics of the situation. Her task was to work with both women individually, interpreting and translating different understandings, experiences and expectations. An important aspect of the work was recognising and highlighting the differentials in Western and ethnically specific values. With both individuals the task was to help them appreciate the other's perspective. Through discussion in the girls' group and with the individual the worker was able to help the young woman and her peers appreciate how minority cultures become insular and inflexible as they struggle to preserve cultural traditions in a hostile environment. With the mother, the worker helped to raise awareness that cultural traditions were subject to change and how patriarchal systems worked to control women. The worker also used her own family and their membership of the community to solicit support for the family in the decision they had taken and to acknowledge the inappropriateness of monocultural values and behavioural norms in a multicultural setting. The outcome of the intervention was that the mother accepted her daughter's choice and agreed that the young people could get married if they were serious about each other after they had completed their undergraduate studies. The young woman agreed to modify her behaviour within community settings to save her mother distress and humiliation.

This example highlights the difficulties workers face in mediating between different cultural systems. On the one hand there is a minority community with its distinctive language, religious and cultural beliefs and prescribed norms of behaviour. However, this exists and is situated within a majority, where individual rights are paramount and the norms of behaviour are quite different. This does not mean that the worker should collude with harmful cultural traditions, but that she acknowledges the differences between generations which arise out of different cultural values. Some young people may choose to identify with the dominant value system without considering the implications that this may have for them and their situation within minority collectivist traditions. They may not have a good understanding of the complex dynamics of the various influences that shape and mould their thoughts and actions. Intervention in such situations needs to focus on interpreting the relative significance of different social systems in the individual's life and facilitating informed decisions.

Some workers might well perceive this to be a matter of individual choice and the right of the young woman to choose her partner. This would be entirely from an individualistic perspective, and they would not be enabling her to make well-informed decisions. The young woman would be at risk of being ostracised by the community if she were seen to be flouting religious and cultural values. The consequences for the entire family would be equally damaging as they would be held responsible for her behaviour and also face rejection and isolation.

For practitioners the issue is about how to promote individual choice at the same time as acknowledging pluralism in cultures and the constraints on the individual. The task for the worker would be to support the mother and the family within the community to challenge the patriarchal systems which control women through notions of respectability and honour. Intervention should also be informed by an understanding of why minorities appear to be resistant to change and to protect traditional values. As Kishwar (1996: 12) explains in relation to India, minority communities in the West have become:

> more culturally rigid than their counterparts in India because they perceive change largely in terms of Westernisation and loss of cultural identity, while those living in India do not view themselves in danger of losing their identity when they adapt to changing times...[such communities, in the West] in name of tradition and cultural identity impose far more repressive norms.

Ejaz (1991), exploring the concept of self-determination and intervention by practitioners within the Indian context suggests that due to the collectivist cultural value of interdependence, users are not threatened by the 'spirit of dependency' and are 'socially open to advice and guidance from others', especially from someone who has greater knowledge either through education or through age and experience. South Asian workers report that this is an important factor when negotiating with parents in supporting young people, and is not construed as interference in personal affairs.

Youth workers are often faced with dilemmas relating to balancing the rights of one individual against those of other people. In resolving such dilemmas the utilitarian premise that the right action is one which promotes the greatest good for the greatest number is often involved (Banks 1995; Smith 1988). In the preceding example, such an approach might have meant disregarding Asha's feelings and prioritising the welfare of her mother and sisters over her own. It is evident that there are no easy solutions to such issues and often workers are left with having to make choices between equally undesirable outcomes.

Loyalty and accountability

The employment of black workers in both mainstream and black-led agencies has also raised distinctive issues of accountability and loyalty – to young people, communities and employers. For example, those that were employed by statutory youth services or other mainstream organisations to promote work with black young people were faced with conflicts between loyalty and accountability to employers and to communities which they were employed to serve. Some of these are similar to those faced by women and lesbian, gay and bisexual workers working with the respective groups of young people. Others resulted from the institutional and structural racism they faced as black workers. In black-led projects that were set up to meet the need of particular communities the issues arose through conflicts between the personal/professional values of workers and the traditional values of the employers.

Two parallel developments have brought about the involvement of black workers in youth work. Following the recognition of the disaffection of black young people (Scarman 1981), funding was made available for local authorities to promote work with black communities and black young people in particular. Local authorities, in complying with the Race Relations Act (1976) and their equal opportunities policies, recruited black workers to extend their services to black young people and communities. The Thompson Report (HMSO 1982), through its recognition of the oppression of black young people and recommendations for their integration, indirectly facilitated the employment of black youth workers in mainstream agencies. Second, through the funding made available, black activists and anti-racist workers formed alliances to establish projects specifically for black young people which were managed and staffed by black people (Jarrett 1989). The Urban Programme, in particular, financed a number of short-term, time-limited projects to meet the 'special needs' of black young people and communities. These special needs were defined in terms of language and culture rather than an acknowledgement of racism and the failure of the system to meet the needs of black citizens. Maina (1989) defines this as 'the culturalisation of race' by local state structures as resources were linked to ethnic and cultural differences in attempting to integrate black groups (Stewart and Whiting 1983). Several Afro-Caribbean and Asian projects were set up to meet the cultural needs of those groups; some of these were specifically for young people.

Black workers in mainstream organisations

The development of youth work and recruitment of black workers raised issues of ethics in the actions taken and the discriminatory effects of practices adopted to counter discrimination. On the one hand, where local authorities and other agencies took a radical approach, positive action was taken through training and apprenticeship schemes that specifically targeted black trainees and workers. As a result, qualified black workers were recruited with experience, knowledge, values and skills to work effectively with black young people. One of the main reasons for appointing black workers was to form 'a bridge between white-dominated institutions and black young people' (Patten 1997: 29). The strengths of black workers were seen as their ability to identify with issues faced by young people, to serve as good role models, and to use their skills and experience to empower young people. This position, despite being one of strength, was also one of vulnerability. As they mediated between the unequal black and white systems and people, this position was in itself precarious. They were perceived to be 'too close to black communities' by employers who questioned their loyalty and professionalism. On the other hand, they were also regarded as 'too close to white institutions' and their loyalty to black communities and young people was also questioned.

A second approach based in liberal multiculturalism was reflected by those agencies who absolved themselves of the responsibility to meet the needs of black young people by appointing black people as youth workers. The 'specialists' appointed were expected to develop work which met the needs of black young people. The ethnicity or 'race' of the worker – being black or Bangladeshi – was the qualification for working with black young people and communities, and this alone was regarded as giving the worker the credentials for practice. In the words of one worker, they were appointed on the 'ticket of culture'. The outcomes of these 'liberal' approaches have proved damaging for both the workers and the young people and communities they were recruited to serve. With limited consideration given to skills and training in youth work, such workers were thrown in at the deep end and expected to sink or swim. Little effort was made once the 'positive action' of appointing black workers had been taken to train and develop them to work more effectively with young people. As one worker commented:

> although I had very little experience in youth work I was appointed because I was black. Seven years on, I have tried to go on courses and undertake training but there has been little support. Cuts in the training budget have meant that I have had to pay myself for some courses that I have identified. I was plodding on, providing mainly leisure activities until I attended the Black Workers' Conference...it was brilliant! I became aware of some really good issue-based work and made really good contacts. It provided an opportunity to discuss some of the real issues facing young people and to identify strategies for working with black people.

Those who survived did so through their commitment to personal and professional development, and not through the responsibility of their employers to staff development and training.

Like their counterparts in social work practice, the workers who came in with knowledge, skills, experience and 'a commitment to fight racism unreservedly' (Patel 1995: 33) found themselves to be marginalised by the agency and other colleagues (including black colleagues) as they were seen as 'too black', 'not objective', 'unprofessional' and 'too close to the black community'. The vulnerability of such workers was further heightened by the fact that other black workers were used against them. As Patel comments, not all black workers act 'in the best interests of racial and social justice, or for the greater good' (ibid.: 33). For some black workers, appointed as a result of liberal policies, 'equal opportunities' became 'equal opportunism'. Such workers reflected individualistic values and were committed only to themselves and their professional advancement. They felt accountable solely to their employers and not to young people or communities. In their professional practice they adopted a 'traditionalist' or 'Western' approach which corresponded to employer expectations. In the case of the former, they justified their employment by demonstrating stereotypical traditional values which were completely at odds with those of young people. Those employed because they were seen to be 'Westernised' and 'progressive' used their professional platform to deny ethnicity and difference and ignored the impact of these on black young people by adopting and advocating the values of the institutions and agencies uncritically. Such practices and outcomes demonstrate how inequality and oppression is reinforced and confirmed by the very strategies used to counter and challenge discrimination and disadvantage (Ben Tovim *et al.* 1992)

Black workers in black-led organisations

The ethical issues faced by youth workers in black-led agencies arise primarily through conflicting values of workers and employers and the multiple roles of practitioners. The historical development of black-led organisations on the basis of language and culture has resulted in division and conflict within and between different groups as they struggled to access limited resources. This has also promoted ethnocentrism within different cultural and religious groups. Some workers employed by specific cultural projects to work with young people as part of the range of services offered report conflicts between agency values and the principles and values that are central to youth work practice. For example, youth workers employed in mosques, mandirs and gurdwaras (like those involved in church-based work) find themselves at odds with employers who are not in favour of promoting equality for women or lesbian and gay young people. One worker mentioned how fundamentalist groups were using young people as vigilantes to hunt for and bring back young women who had left home against parental wishes to pursue higher education or who were fleeing due to violence in the home.

Ethical dilemmas are also presented by the multiple roles that workers occupy (Banks 1997). Collectivist values compound these dilemmas further through different role expectations – by young people, by communities, other workers and other communities. Conflicts occur when these different roles as a practitioner and professional and a member of a particular community are brought to play in a specific situation. The case of Asha cited earlier is a good example of the complexity of the position black workers face. Another worker shared her experiences in a similar situation:

> I was working with a young woman who was going out with a married man from our community. The wife knew that I was a youth worker and approached me for help. I was already working with the young woman who was regular member of the girls' group. As a member of the community I knew about the man's reputation and that he was abusing the young woman as well as his wife…it was a nightmare…made worse when he threatened me and other members in my family about interfering in his personal affairs.

In this situation the worker is caught up in an extremely difficult situation. As a youth work practitioner she has to work with issues of autonomy and self-determination as well as her professional assessment of the young woman's welfare. As a member of a partic-ular community and a practitioner working within that community, she is known to all the parties concerned, who have their own perceptions and expectations of her different roles. This also heightens her vulnerability as a practitioner in bringing together the personal and professional roles. Such situations are not uncommon among black workers where issues of loyalty and accountability to the community are brought into play alongside their roles and responsibilities as youth and community workers. In resolving these issues workers have to critically assess their roles in relation to the community and their profession. These need to be explicated in light of the workers' own ethical principles and values and their professional values.

Moving beyond ethnocentric values and ethics

Working with diverse constituencies of young people one cannot assume universalistic perspectives which homogenise differences and confirm the dominance of majority norms. Practitioners need to move beyond simplistic explanations that polarise Western and non-Western, black and white, traditional and Westernised, individualist and collectivist and provide the space for fusion and complication between these in acknowledgement and validation of the complexity and diversity of young people's lives. Mark Smith, in initiating the discussion on the ethics underpinning work with young people in a multi-ethnic context, suggests that the central task for the youth workers is to enable young people to develop the ability to think critically in order to:

> to address their own culture, to own their own experiences, and hence to speak in their own voices...people must also learn what is good, they must learn what values are central to human life and well being and how such values are transmitted and tortured in the interests of the powerful. Finally, people must learn about the structural and ideological forces which influence and restrict their lives.
>
> (Smith 1988: 114)

The task of the youth worker, therefore, is to facilitate the process through which black young people are able critically to evaluate and identify the values that are fundamental to their welfare. What is important then, is the ability of workers to move between different social and cultural systems, to relate to different constituencies of people: black and white, disabled and able-bodied, lesbian, gay, bisexual and heterosexual, women and men, and across different social classes. In other words, they have to become what Giroux has termed 'border crossers':

> educators have to become more than intellectual tourists. We must move into the spheres, where we take up different contexts, geographies, different languages, of otherness and recognise the otherness in ourselves...we also have to recognise the partiality of our views.
>
> (Giroux 1994: 167–8)

The acknowledgement of the partiality of different experiences and views is crucial to this process. Such an acknowledgement may be problematic from majorities, who through their dominance have pushed minorities into occupying such a position. The practice examples cited earlier illustrate how black workers have usually worked from this basic premise, recognising the partiality of their understandings and values in relation to those of black and white young people and communities. Patricia Hill Collins (1990: 236) suggests that this positioning may be possible when 'partiality and not universality is the condition of being heard'. The core purpose of youth work – to promote the self-determination and self-emancipation of young people through collective action (NYA 1997) – provides the opportunity for this condition to be imposed on all people that come together with this objective. In advocating this positioning we can draw from the work of black feminists who have attempted to address issues of essentialism and universalism in women's groups. Nira Yuval-Davies (1994) proposes the notion of transversalism, as distinct from universalism, based on such a partial positioning. It is based on two related concepts of 'rooting' and 'shifting', each individual is rooted in her own identity and culture and shifts in order to put herself in the position of the other.

With reference to an inclusive framework for ethics and values in youth work we can propose transversal values and ethics which are of relevance to all groups of young people. Practitioners may be rooted in their own perspectives and values, but shift in order to place themselves in the position of the user or young person with different values. What is important is that in shifting one does not lose one's own rooting and values:

> All people can learn to centre in another experience, validate it, judge it by its own standards without need of comparison or need to adopt the framework as their own...one has no need to de-centre anyone in order to centre someone else.
>
> (Brown 1989, quoted in Yuval-Davis 1994: 193)

This is learning which dominant groups will have to derive from the experiences of people whose perspectives and values they have historically de-centred and denied. To move beyond ethnocentric values requires this partial positioning from all groups that come together for collective action – majorities and minorities.

Bibliography

Ahmad, B. (1990) *Black Perspectives in Social Work*, London: Venture Press.

Ahmed, S. (1986) 'Cultural racism in work with Asian women and girls', *Social Work with Black Children and their Families*, London: Batsford.

Anthias, F. and Yuval-Davis, N. (1992) *Racialised Boundaries: Race, Nation, Gender and Class and the Anti-racist Struggle*, London: Routledge.

Banks, S. (1995) *Ethics and Values in Social Work*, Basingstoke: Macmillan.

—— (1997) 'The dilemmas of intervention', in J. Roche and S. Tucker (eds) *Youth in Society: Contemporary Theory, Policy and Practice*, London: Open University/Sage.

Ben-Tovim, G., Gabriel, J., Law, I. and Stredder, K. (1992) 'A political analysis of local struggles for racial equality', in P. Braham, A. Rattansi, and R. Skellington (eds) *Racism and Anti-racism: Inequalities, Opportunities and Policies*, London: Open University/Sage.

Brah, A. (1992) 'Difference, diversity and differentiation' in J. Donald and A. Rattansi (eds) *'Race', Culture and Difference*, London: Open University/Sage.

Chodorow, N. (1989) *Feminism and Psychoanalytic Theory*, New Haven: Yale University Press.

Collins, P. H. (1991) *Black Feminist Thought: Knowledge, Consciousness and the Politics of Empowerment*, London: Routledge.

Ejaz, F. (1991) 'Self-determination: lessons to be learned from social work practice in India', *British Journal of Social Work* 21: 127–42.

Gilligan, C. (1982) *In a Different Voice*, Cambridge MA: Harvard University Press.

Giroux, H. A. (1994) *Disturbing Pleasures*, London: Routledge.

Gordon, P. and Klug, F. (1986) *New Right, New Racism*, London: Searchlight.

Hall, S. (1992) 'New ethnicities' in J. Donald, and A. Rattansi (eds) *Race, Culture and Difference*, London: Open University/Sage.

HMSO (1982) *Experience and Participation: Report of the Review Group on the Youth Service in England* (The Thompson Report) London: HMSO.

Husband, C. (1995) 'The morally active practitioner and the ethics of anti-racist work', in R. Hugman and D. Smith (eds) *Ethical Issues in Social Work*, London: Routledge.

Jarrett, M. (1989) *Efficiency and Effectiveness of the Black Voluntary Sector.* London: NCVO.

Jewson, N. and Mason, D. (1992) 'The theory and practice of equal opportunities policies' in P. Braham, A. Rattansi and R. Skellington (eds) *Racism and Anti-racism: Inequalities, Opportunities and Policies*, London: Open University/Sage.

Kagitcibasi, C. (1996) *Family and Human Development Across Cultures: A View from the Other Side*, New Jersey: Lawrence Erlsbaum.

—— (1997) 'Individualism and collectivism' in J. W. Berry, M. H. Segall and C. Kagitcibasi (eds) *Handbook of Cross-Cultural Psychology: Social Behaviour and Applications*, Boston: Allyn and Bacon.

Kishwar, M. (1996) 'Who am I? Living identities vs acquired ones', *Manushi* 94: 6–17.

Maclaren, P. (1995) *Critical Pedagogy and Predatory Culture*, London: Routledge.

Mama, A. (1989) *The Hidden Struggle: Statutory and Voluntary Sector Responses to Violence Against Women in the Home*, London: London Race and Housing Research Unit.

—— (1995) *Race, Gender and Subjectivity*, London: Routledge.

Markus, H. R. and Kitayama, S. (eds) (1991) 'Culture and the self: implications for cognition, emotion and motivation', *Psychological Review* 98(2): 224–53.

Marsella, A. J., DeVos, G. and Hsu, F. L. K. (1985) *Culture and Self: Asian and Western Perspectives*, New York: Tavistock.

Mishra, R. C. (1994) 'Individualism and collectivism orientations across generations' in U. Kim, H. C. Triandis, C. Kagitcibasi, S-C. Choi and G. Yoon (eds) *Individualism and Collectivism: Theory, Method and Applications*, Thousand Oaks CA: Sage.

Narayan, U. (1989) 'The project of feminist epistemology: perspectives from a non-Western feminist' in A. Jaggar and S. Bordo (eds) *Gender/Body/Knowledge: Feminist Reconstructions of Being and Knowing*, New Brunswick NJ: Rutgers University Press.

National Youth Agency (1997) *Mapping the Youth Work Sector: A Summary Report*, Leicester: NYA.

Patel, N. (1995) 'In search of the holy grail' in R. Hugman and D. Smith (eds) *Ethical Issues in Social Work*, London: Routledge.

Patten, P. (1997) 'Racism and respect: black pride, black youth and black workers' in D. Garratt, Roche, J. and Tucker, S. (eds) *Changing Experiences of Youth,* London: Open University/Sage.

Scarman, Lord (1981) *The Brixton Disorders 10–12 April 1981*, London: HMSO.

Sinha, D. and Tripathi, R. C. (1994) 'Individualism in a collectivist culture: a case of co-existence of opposites' in U. Kim, H. C. Triandis, C. Kagitcibasi, S-C. Choi and G. Yoon (eds) *Individualism and Collectivism: Theory, Method and Applications*, Thousand Oaks CA: Sage.

Smith, M. (1988) *Developing Youth Work: Informal Education, Mutual Aid and Popular Practice*, Milton Keynes: Open University Press.

Smith, P. B. and Schwartz, S. H. (1997) 'Values', in J. W. Berry, M. H. Segall and C. Kagitcibasi (eds) *Handbook of Cross-Cultural Psychology: Social Behaviour and Applications*, Boston: Allyn and Bacon.

Smith, P. B. and Bond, M. H. (1993) *Social Psychology Across Cultures: Analysis and Perspectives*, London: Harvester Wheatsheaf.

Stewart, M. and Whiting, G. (1983) *Ethnic Minorities and the Urban Programme*, Bristol: University of Bristol, School of Advanced Urban Studies.

Woolett, A., Marshall, H., Nicolson, P. and Dosanjh, N. (1994) 'Asian women's ethnic identity: the impact of gender and context in the accounts of women bringing up children in east London' in K. Bhavnani and A. Phoenix (eds) *Shifting Identities and Shifting Racisms: A Feminist and Psychology Reader*, London: Sage.

Yuval-Davis, N. (1994) 'Women, Ethnicity and Empowerment' in K. Bhavnani and A. Phoenix (eds) *Shifting Identities, Shifting Racisms: A Feminist and Psychology Reader*, London: Sage.

9

THE YOUTH WORKER AS CONFIDANTE

Issues of welfare and trust

Sue Morgan and Sarah Banks

Introduction

Youth workers often form close relationships with young people and are sought out as adults who can help with personal problems. Often young people discuss their feelings and actions with youth workers and expect or request that these discussions are kept confidential. Dilemmas arise for youth workers when the information they are given is of a serious nature – when the worker is unsure of how to handle it, when the young person or other people may be in difficulty or danger, or when illegal activities are reported. Youth workers are also party to information about people's activities that they overhear or observe during their work. Some of this information may simply be known about; some may be recorded in files. There are issues around what types of information should be regarded as confidential; to whom should confidentiality be extended; what should be recorded; who should have access to records; in what circumstances should information be revealed; should young people be informed when confidentiality is breached?

Although 'confidentiality' is much discussed in youth work, it is relatively under-explored. This chapter will consider the meanings of confidentiality, how it applies in youth work in general, and in a variety of situations often encountered by youth workers. Since little has been written on confidentiality in youth work, we will draw on the literature from the other welfare professions – particularly social work and counselling. Although there are many commonalities, it is important to bear in mind that the roles of youth workers are very different from those of counsellors or social workers and therefore give rise to different types of issues.

The nature of confidentiality

Confidentiality is essentially about trust. It is usually associated with entrusting someone with a secret. Since the nature of a secret is that it is hidden, and few people know about it, then confidentiality is about trusting someone not to reveal this information. In the literature on professional ethics, it is often linked with the idea of privacy and rights of service users to determine who should know information about them, especially information they have given to the professional for a particular purpose (Beauchamp and Childress 1994: 418–30; Marshall 1991; Rhodes 1986: 56–82). For example, the code of ethics for social work (BASW 1996) states that social workers:

> will recognise that information clearly entrusted for one purpose should not be used for another purpose without sanction. They will respect the privacy of clients and others with whom they come into contact and confidential information gained in their relationships with them.

There are several arguments about why professional confidentiality is important. Bok (1982) suggests it can be justified with reference to four ethical principles: human autonomy regarding personal information; respect for relationships; respect for promises; and the benefit of confidentiality to society and to people needing help. As Rhodes (1986: 62–4) points out, the first three principles are interrelated and could be categorised as a Kantian justification of confidentiality – with a focus on the respect and dignity owed to each individual person. The fourth principle stresses the usefulness of confidentiality to society. If confidentiality did not exist, people would not share information about issues and problems and therefore not receive the help they need. If no one knew whether they could trust anyone to keep a secret, then the world would become a more suspicious, individualised unfriendly place. This is a utilitarian argument, justifying confidentiality in relation to it being in the interests of the greatest good of the greatest number of people.

What is confidential information?

Often the information referred to is specified as that 'given by the clients to social workers' (Shardlow 1995: 67) or 'disclosures by the patient or client to the professional' (Wilson 1978: 2). This might be interpreted as implying that confidentiality only applies to information actively given by a client or service user to the professional worker. Yet this is a rather narrow interpretation of 'confidential information'. If the whole professional relationship is regarded as based on trust, then the idea of 'entrusting information' may be extended to include information that the professional gains about a client in the course of their professional relationship regardless of whether it is directly given to the professional. An example from medicine illustrates this point. A doctor may come to know matters about a patient's treatment, illness and diagnosis which have not been revealed by the patient. These would nevertheless be regarded as confidential between the patient and doctor. In the case of youth work, the privileged access of workers to intimate, personal aspects of young people's lives may not be as great. But it is certainly there. In considering what counts as confidential information, it is important to go beyond the information directly communicated by young people.

Biestek gives a useful analysis of different types of confidential information in relation to social work. He defines confidential information as:

> a fact or a condition, or the knowledge thereof, pertaining to a person's private life which is normally hidden from the eyes of others.
>
> (Biestek 1961: 123)

He then divides this into three categories:

1   The natural secret is information which, if revealed, would 'defame, injure, or unjustly sadden' someone. Everyone (for example, friends, relatives, strangers or a professional) has a duty to preserve this secret. In the case of professional social and youth workers, it covers information which may have become known by a worker unofficially outside the professional relationship.

2   The promised secret is where the confidante gives a promise, after the secret information has been revealed, not to divulge it. The information may include defamatory facts as in the natural secret, or non-defamatory information of a personal nature.

3   The entrusted secret is information given with the previous
    explicit or implicit understanding that it will not be revealed.
    The subject matter may or may not include a natural secret and
    the implicit/explicit contract between the two people binds the
    confidante to secrecy even if the information is not defamatory.
    In the context of professional social work, or youth work, it is
    the entrusted secret that is most commonly encountered.

It seems relatively uncontroversial to regard the entrusted and
promised secrets as types of confidential information. Biestek's
account of the natural secret, however, is more problematic. There
are two ways in which a worker may come to know a natural secret.
The first is in the course of professional work – for example, in a
youth work setting by listening, watching or being told something
by a third party. This is clearly a case where confidentiality would
be expected if the information is of a 'defamatory' character. The
second is outside the professional relationship – for example at a
party, or when out shopping on a Saturday. Although Biestek
classifies this as 'confidential information', it might be more appropriate to regard it as 'private information' if there was no relationship
of trust involved at the time when the information was gained. For
example, imagine a case where a worker learns during conversation
at a dinner party that the father of a young woman who attends the
worker's youth club is in prison for drug dealing. The person who
revealed this information was not aware that the youth worker knew
the young woman, and did not assume or request confidentiality.
Therefore, although the youth worker is the recipient of sensitive
information of a personal nature, it does not make sense to regard
her as a confidante. The worker may well decide it would be wrong
to reveal this information to fellow workers or club members. But
this would more accurately be characterised as respecting the young
woman's right to privacy, not confidentiality. This may seem merely
a semantic point, but it is not. How the worker construes the nature
of the information and the circumstances in which it is received may
influence how she decides to use it. If the worker thinks of herself
as in the role of a worker even when at a dinner party, and regards
the information as confidential, then she may feel perfectly justified
in informing her supervisor, fellow workers or recording it in a file.
Because, for a youth worker employed by an agency, confidentiality
usually means secret within the team or agency, by regarding it as
private information she would keep it to herself.

Applying the principle of confidentiality

Bond's (1995) research on confidentiality in multi-disciplinary teams working with people with HIV found at least four interpretations of confidentiality. Similar variations would no doubt be found in youth work. It is notable that such variations were found in HIV work as this is an area where professionals are highly aware of issues around confidentiality and they have been much debated. The four meanings Bond (1995: 6–7) identified were:

- secrecy: everything disclosed is secret to the people present;
- confidential disclosures remain the property of the person who made the disclosure who must therefore be consulted before that information is communicated to others;
- confidential disclosures are given on trust to be used in the best interests of the person who made the disclosure to someone who needs to know that information in order to further the best interests;
- confidentiality entails following the practice laid down in agency policy and by the appropriate professional body.

This list of interpretations highlights two important points. First, how far does the confidentiality extend? We talk about the worker as 'confidante' which implies it is a one-to-one relationship between the worker and the person entrusting the information. But this is not generally the case for professionals working in the health and welfare field where it is rare that confidentiality is confined to one person. In many cases, confidentiality extends to the worker and their supervisor, or the team to which the worker belongs, or to the whole agency, or to the agency and other professionals who work with that agency. This will depend on the practices and policies of particular agencies and workers. Even a counsellor in private practice will usually have supervision – indeed the code of practice for professional counsellors requires this (BAC 1993). Youth workers who are employed by an agency, whether this is a small voluntary agency or a large local authority, will also expect to receive supervision, discuss problematic issues with colleagues and in certain circumstances (particularly suspected child sexual abuse) will be required to report serious matters to their line managers or beyond. The difference between a counsellor in private practice and an employee of an organisation is that in the case of the former the confidential information does not have to be revealed to anyone else and no action need be taken on the information received (except in very specific situations such as the prevention of terrorism, where it is legally required, see Bond 1993: 127–9). The private practice counsellor is working for the client and the client should be in control of the information, respecting the core principle of client autonomy. However, in the case of workers employed by agencies, usually the worker is working to the agency's agenda as well as that of the client. Part of this agenda may be about promoting the welfare of the client regardless of what they would choose themselves (e.g. preventing suicide, injury), protecting other clients (e.g. reporting an attempted theft), or serving the public interest (e.g. reporting crimes).

This leads to the second issue regarding when is it justified not to promise confidentiality, or, if it has been promised or expected, when to break it. If we pay attention to the first question, there may be less cases arising when confidentiality has to be broken. Interestingly, a lot of the discussion by youth workers relates to the issue of breaking confidentiality – ignoring the question of the types of occasions when confidentiality should not be offered or assumed in the first place. Most definitions of confidentiality and statements of principles of codes of ethics outline when confidentiality does not apply. For example, the BASW (1996) code of ethics states that the social worker will only divulge information entrusted in the professional relationship with the consent of the client or informant except where:

> there is clear evidence of serious danger to the client, worker, other persons or the community or in other circumstances, judged exceptional, on the basis of professional considera-tion and consultation.

This gives workers permission either not to offer confidentiality, or to break it in these cases. If an agency has a clear policy on when confidentiality cannot be assured this makes it easier for workers. The agency may also have policies about the types of information which the worker has a duty to reveal. Workers may face dilemmas in relation to whether they should follow their agency's policy on confidentiality, which may require them to reveal personal or defamatory information to their line managers, or whether, in the interests of the freedom or welfare of the young person they will not divulge this information.

Confidentiality and the youth worker's role

So far we have used the literature particularly from social work and counselling to illuminate the nature of confidentiality in a professional context. We will now consider some of the specific features of the youth worker's role which may differentiate it from these other welfare professions. The youth worker has already been characterised as an informal educator (see Chapter 1). Youth workers do not tend to have formal one-to-one encounters with individual young people in the way that social workers and counsellors do. So there is less chance to explain the nature of confidentiality to young people, or to establish a 'contract' setting out expectations. Because youth workers work informally and often in a relaxed way, they may not be perceived by the young people as 'professionals', or as part of a large-scale bureaucracy with a plethora of responsibilities and accountabilities. They may be perceived more as a 'friend' than a professional worker. There may be much more room for misunderstanding about the nature of the relationship and the extent of confidentiality than there would be in a young person's encounter with a social worker. It may more easily be assumed that the first interpretation of confidentiality identified by Bond applies – that everything revealed is secret to the people present.

Youth workers do not generally regard themselves as working with 'clients'. They work with the young people who happen to turn up at their project, or young people they encounter in the street. It may be very unclear for some youth workers who counts as a 'service user'. A detached youth worker may have conversations or hang around with a whole host of young people in the street and pick up information. Should information picked up about abuse or crime be kept confidential or revealed? If a worker is found to be a 'grass' then this will spoil the trust they have built up with groups of young people. Although this is equally true for counsellors and social workers, it is particularly significant in youth work with its informal approach.

The other main difference from social work and counselling is that youth work has a much more radical educational focus, with a greater emphasis on working for societal change, as well as personal development. Criticisms of counselling and other forms of therapy often rest on the fact that they are premised on the assumption that everyone is responsible for their own situation in life. This locates power in the individual and ignores structural oppression. It treats pain in private rather than making issues public. So whilst people who have been abused, raped or hurt can be helped by counselling to feel better, this does nothing to stop such atrocities. Regardless of whether we think counselling is individually helpful, socially beneficial or positively harmful, youth work starts from a different position, with a different set of values that encompasses the challenging of structural oppression as well as promoting individual autonomy and welfare.

The implications for youth workers' approach to confidentiality are that it is more likely that other values and principles – such as promoting equality or challenging oppression – will conflict with the principle of respecting confidentiality. Confidentiality is important in maintaining trust and respecting individual rights to self-determination and privacy, but the youth worker will also regard it as important that, for example, abusers are prevented from exploiting young people, that issues of drug dealing are openly discussed and tackled, that bullying and harassment are recognised and prevented. As Churchill and Honning (1997: 66) state, in the context of sexual violence:

> safety and sexual violence is a community issue, it's everyone's responsibility and the community can support victims by acknowledging the issues and providing support.

This gives youth workers a responsibility to have conversations with young people which enable them to understand that their difficulties may not be their fault and that they may be rooted in broader social issues. Finally, youth workers, like social workers, but unlike most counsellors, do have a public responsibility for the welfare of the young people with whom they work. This means there are occasions when the agency requires confidentiality cannot be given or should be broken – when young people or others are in danger or being harmed.

Ethical dilemmas for youth workers relating to confidentiality

Youth work organisations have only recently begun to develop policies on confidentiality and pay attention to it in training. It is becoming more of an issue now partly because a small but growing number of projects are being established to work with individuals in difficulty – offering advice, support or even counselling. The growth of multi-agency working tends to highlight the need for confidentiality policies if, for example, a youth work agency routinely works with the police, social workers or teachers. There is also an increased awareness of sexual abuse and procedures which require that the different professional groups work together and that youth workers report cases of suspected abuse to the Social Services Department.

There are many ways dilemmas about confidentiality manifest themselves in youth work. When and to whom should records or files be shown? Does 'gossip' amongst youth workers and volunteers (who may be members of the local community and pass on the information outside) about details of young people's personal lives constitute a breach of confidentiality? But the types of issues about which youth workers hold confidential information which they regard as most serious and cause them the most soul-searching are those where they may know a young person is involved in something which might cause them, or other people, serious harm and/or which is against the law and is against the public interest. Youth workers invariably mention instances relating to drug use, crime, under-age sex and sexual and physical abuse. The dilemmas raised in these situations usually relate to balancing the young person's rights – to privacy; to freedom to determine their own actions; to have their confidence respected (derived from Kantian principles), against the rights or interests of particular others or society as a whole (utilitarian considerations). Rhodes (1986: 64) argues that the principle of 'protecting society' may often outweigh the individual's rights to autonomy and privacy. However, the breaking of confidence is regarded as serious because it usually involves a betrayal of trust, or at least the potential loss of trust of the young person or young people being worked with.

Confidentiality and harm reduction: young people and drugs

Conversations between youth workers and young people about drugs are commonplace. Young people often want to talk privately about their levels of consumption and behaviour whilst under the influence. Young people will only have these kinds of conversations if they are confident that the worker is not going to report them to the police, their parents or their schools. However, there are situations where it is impossible for youth workers to keep confidences about drugs – for example, if the worker becomes concerned for the immediate safety of young people and judges that they are incapable of making sound decisions. If young people are obviously in danger, having taken too much of a certain drug or having a bad reaction, a youth worker will probably consider their plea for confidentiality less important than the need to save their lives, and so inform parents or take them to hospital. If the danger is more long term, and if the young person has consistently failed to seek help, then workers may consider it their duty to inform parents. The age of the young person is significant and would affect workers' judgement about their responsibility to the parents or carers.

The duty to keep confidence is also balanced by considerations for the safety of others. Workers may well come to hear whom the dealers in a local community are. Difficulties in keeping this confidential might arise if the dealer is known to be unscrupulous – for example, cutting drugs with more dangerous substances, dealing to children, or being involved in acts of violence to procure drugs or pay for them. Reporting dealers whom the wider community may perceive as providing a useful service to them makes it difficult for workers to maintain relationships or even their presence in this community. It makes them inaccessible to the very people whose needs they could most usefully serve.

The following example was recounted by a youth worker who had been working informally with a group of young people engaged in illegal activities. This is a case where the worker had information that he had picked up in the course of his work (a natural secret).

> A youth worker employed to work in a youth centre in an inner city area had been doing some detached work with a group of about twenty young people aged 14–20 who congregated on street corners near the centre. They had a passion for rave music, and over half of the group admitted to using drugs (mainly Ecstasy and LSD). The group complained of boredom, so a contract was drawn up with them enabling them to use a room in the centre twice a week to play their music. They agreed that no illegal substances would be brought into the centre and that they would not come in under the influence of drugs. With the odd exception this agreement was kept, and the worker began working with a sub-group on issues around drugs. Problems emerged when a drug dealer known to some of the young people started hanging around outside the centre. Due to his close contacts with the young people, the worker had information which would be likely to lead to the arrest of the dealer. Colleagues and the majority of the members of the centre's management committee urged the

worker to go to the police. The worker knew that this would mean losing contact with the young people and being labelled as a 'grass'. He felt he had been making some headway with them on harm reduction strategies.

This case involved conflict between a worker's view about what he should do (maintaining the trust of a small group of individuals), and the views of others in his agency (catching a drug dealer in the broader public interest). Whilst the fact of the dealer hanging around was public knowledge (the management committee members knew about this), it was the details of his activities known by the worker which would make a difference to whether he was caught by the police or not. What the worker eventually did might not only depend on how strongly he stuck to his principle of confidentiality, but also whether he thought the police would actually catch the dealer and how much good that would do in terms of reducing drug use in the area compared with the harm that would be done to the productive work he was doing with this group of young people.

Confidentiality and collusion: young people and crime

As trusted adults, known to have regular wages, it is not unusual for young people to offer youth workers stolen goods, or perhaps the services of shoplifters. If youth workers were to report to the police the thefts that they were aware of, their presence in communities would not be tolerated. The situations that are likely to incline the worker towards reporting young people's involvement in theft are when it threatens someone else's safety. Being told of a violent theft, having happened or being planned, may be justification for breaking confidence. Hearing of the thrill a young person may attest to in 'creeping', that is, burgling a house (perhaps a bedroom) while the occupants are asleep, might persuade some workers to report them immediately to the police. Others may engage in conversations aiming to deter young people from such activity and only report them at a later date if they continue to carry out such crimes.

Frequently the people who make up the communities with which youth workers are involved live on low incomes. Education about the structural inequality of society is a crucial concern for youth workers, and the discussions in which they involve young people have important implications. Workers and young people are acutely aware of the pressure brought to bear by consumerism, the hardship experienced by many young people and their families and how this is compounded by feeling, for example, that they ought to be wearing expensive designer clothes. There will be a very wide range of opinions among different workers regarding work with young people's feelings of inadequacy caused by poverty. The following example was given by an experienced youth worker:

> A young woman had worked closely with a local youth project over a period of two years. She was a single mother with little family support. She was enthusiastic about undertaking training to become involved with the project as a volunteer. As she grew to trust the worker more, she informed the worker that she was part of a shoplifting network, and asked the worker if she had a shopping list of goods which could be provided for less than 25 per cent of the actual cost. The worker declined the offer but did not report the young woman to the police. The young woman went on to gain part time employment as a youth worker. Several years later she was convicted along with several others of theft involving violence. The youth worker was concerned that her own expressions of anger and sympathy about the injustice of poverty might have been interpreted by the young woman as sanctioning her involvement in theft.

Most workers would agree that it is wrong to be involved in or advocate theft, or to receive stolen goods. This is important in that it demonstrates to the people they work with not that they are morally superior, but that their dialogue on the issue is not influenced by their own self-interest. This links with Jeffs and Smith's (1996: 52–3) notion of the 'moral authority' of youth workers, who serve as role models for young people and should therefore practise what they preach. In this case the worker refused the stolen goods, decided it was not appropriate to report the matter to the police, but may not have been clear enough to the young woman concerned that it was not acceptable for volunteer or paid youth workers to be involved in theft. By keeping illegal or morally wrong activities confidential, a worker may give a message to young people that these activities are acceptable. It is important, therefore, to see confidentiality in the wider context of the youth work role. This involves developing young people's trust in the worker not just as someone who will not 'grass', but also as someone whose opinions are to be respected, who will be listened to and who therefore can engage in conversations exploring difficult issues.

Confidentiality and 'private pain': issues of sexual abuse and suicide

Sexual abuse is an issue which is surrounded by apprehension and fear. It is an issue where youth workers' responses are guided directly by their employers as part of the child protection procedures. All local authorities and many voluntary agencies have very clear policies requiring workers to report any cases of suspected child abuse. For example, the child protection literature produced by North Yorkshire County Council (1989: 10.4) to direct youth workers' actions around issues of child abuse states:

> The safety and feelings of a young person come first. If a young person tells you about abuse, or if you suspect it has happened – you must report.

When youth workers consider reporting abuse it is usually with the well-being of the young person paramount. Uncertainty can cloud the issue; fear of repercussions for inappropriate responses looms large. Some workers fear that if the young person is lying, then they too may be accused of abuse. Accusations of abuse, even when unsubstantiated, have the power to wreck youth workers' lives and careers (Nicholls 1995: 163). For some workers the employer's requirement to report the case will be sufficient as to present no dilemma and they will simply see it as their duty. For others, a dilemma is created because the young person was unaware of the youth worker's inability to keep their confidence. If they had known, they would not have given the information. Regulations often warn youth workers against promising confidentiality. This presents a difficult decision relating to the point in the conversation when the worker tells the young person that they cannot keep the confidence.

Some may not tell them at all, waiting until after the young person has gone before informing their line manager or Social Services. This can be criticised as irresponsible, making the situation easier for the worker by avoiding a difficult conversation, and giving the young person no choice in how the situation is approached. A worker following this line of action also loses the chance to inform the young person of the way the procedures work and what will happen. It contradicts the youth work commitment to the empowerment of young people.

Other workers may develop an agreement with the young person about confidentiality. Any circumstances in which this might change would be identified at the time of making that agreement. In youth work practice, in the instance of a young person coming to talk about their private problems, this would involve making clear at the very beginning of the conversation what the worker's constraints on keeping confidentiality are. The City of Newcastle (1996) requires that young people have an informed choice:

> Where a child or young person begins to disclose to you, you must inform them of the procedures that you must follow to allow them to make an informed decision as to whether to continue the conversation.

This attempts to empower the young person and aim for a position where the worker will only receive disclosures from young people who want the worker to report the abuse to Social Services. This gives the young person choice about what they reveal and hopefully a larger say in determining their own future. However, it also implies that the system designed to safeguard the young person may not be implemented and the abuse may continue.

Many experienced youth workers doubt the effectiveness of the child protection procedures in safeguarding the well-being of young people. The hope is that the child protection legislation will protect both the young people and the professionals working with them, that abuse will stop and the perpetrator will be dealt with by the legal system in a way that helps deter others from committing similar crimes, and that throughout this youth workers will be able to maintain relationships with the young people which educate them about and support them through the process. Experience shows that this does not always happen. Taylor-Browne (1997) argues that these strategies fail to address the needs, identified by survivors and their organisations, of children suffering sexual abuse. Only 15 per cent of original referrals go on to the child protection register (Parton et al. 1997: 217). This means that no matter what youth workers judge to have happened, they are not entitled to diagnose abuse: even if they report an actual disclosure, this is regarded only as suspected abuse. Young people sometimes withdraw disclosures made to youth workers when faced with the more formal structure of Social Services.

The following is an account of a dilemma faced by an unqualified youth worker asked to keep a confidence about sexual abuse, which was further complicated by a young woman's expressed intention to commit suicide.

A youth worker was working in a busy youth club on a normal youth club evening. She was approached by a 15-year-old girl, Jan, in the coffee bar who was obviously in a state of distress. The youth worker took her into a quiet room. From that initial contact Jan swore the worker to secrecy. Jan revealed to the worker over several weeks that during the past year she had been raped four times by her father and was now pregnant by him. She had also decided to commit suicide as a way out of the situation. The youth worker talked through the issues with Jan, suggesting various options for help and that suicide was not the best way out. However, Jan continued to refuse to consider any professional help, and insisted that the worker should not tell anyone.

This is an example of an entrusted secret – where the worker explicitly agreed to keep the confidence at the start of the conversation. This makes it particularly difficult for the worker to break the confidence. It also places a great burden on the worker, who may feel as though she is the only source of support available to this young person. But feelings such as this can result in potentially dangerous situations. It could be argued that by not reporting the conversations to the worker's line manager, the youth worker exceeded the limit of her role. It is possible in cases like this to end up in a position of collusion with a young person which contributes to the young person feeling responsible for the situation or the continuation of the abuse.

There are additional pressures if the young person threatens suicide. Workers may feel that they have the responsibility for the young person's life. The worker may consider that the duty to preserve the young person's life outweighs the duty to stop the abuse by reporting it. Knowledge of the issue of suicide may help to counteract pressure and guide the worker to seek help. Hill (1995), in her research on suicidal young people, identified that the desire to die coexists with the desire to live and be helped. She provides a scale by which the lay person can assess the suicide risk, and urges those workers in contact with suicidal young people to talk about it with them rather than be afraid that such talk will provoke them into action. Bass and Davis (1988) detail a suicide prevention plan that abuse survivors can put together when they are feeling that they want to live in order to prepare for times when they feel that they wish to die. Bond (1993) argues that the need to stop someone committing suicide is grounds for seeking professional help and this can be more important than the need to keep confidentiality.

Youth workers sometimes respond inappropriately to young people's crises. There are grim stories about workers who gave suicidal young people their phone numbers so they could be called at any time of the day and night, without really considering the implications. There are those who said they would always be there and then had to go out, and those who promised they would be able to make it all right but could not. An accurate understanding of the limitations of the role of the youth worker, and of the worker's skills is vital. It could be argued that any worker in a position where a young person has disclosed information about a potentially dangerous situation should always share this with a colleague or supervisor. The details of the situation can be discussed without the identity of the young person being revealed. Having no confidence in the line manager or supervisor's ability is not sufficient reason for workers to keep the information to themselves. Abusers thrive on secrets and it is easy to become sucked into the manipulative power plays into which abused young people have become embroiled.

It is important that workers develop an understanding of the dynamics of their own reactions and motives when they feel that a young person needs their help. In situations where workers' feelings can run high, it is important to separate their own feelings from those of the young people they work with. Mander (1997: 35) writes of counsellors: 'the image of the good shepherd associates easily with the Pied Piper, the false prophet, the charismatic fanatic'. Sanders (1996: 43) argues that the harmful side of the motive to help can be the desire for dependency. The helping relationship can be distorted to meet the needs of the helper. Similarly, if the helper has experience of a past emotionally painful trauma they may have gained personal strength from the experience and be more sensitive to others in a similar situation, or they could be over sensitive as their emotional pain is unresolved, and they use contact with the clients to try and resolve their own trauma.

Developing ethical practice

Focusing on the question of violating confidentiality about sexual abuse highlights key areas of preparation with regard to both abuse and other issues where confidentiality is important. Predicting that the situation may occur in the future, work can be carried out that might beneficially impact upon the point of crisis. Working with young people to help them identify their support networks reduces the level of dependency the young person has on the relationship with the youth worker. Promoting the work of the Samaritans, Childline and other agencies who are able to keep confidences directs young people to places they can have confidential discussions whilst trying to decide upon a considered course of action. Fostering debate about the nature of confidentiality informs young people's expectations of workers. Clear communication and agreed systems between workers in the same organisation help clarify sources of support, supervision and courses of action. Developing sound working knowledge of agency guidelines and procedures and building relationships with the staff of Social Services and other agencies at a local level shapes workers' understanding of how scenarios may unfold. Having useful resources available to give to young people may help allay their sense of isolation and workers' sense of powerlessness.

Some projects have developed policies on confidentiality and have identified the need to display information. This gives young people a chance to consider the issue before they say anything to a worker. The development of such policy is a lengthy process and there is a tendency once it is completed to consider the issue adequately covered. If they are to be meaningful and effective, workers need to discuss and debate issues and develop and modify policies and practice as they discover new dilemmas. It is also important to communicate the project's requirements and ways of working to other agencies who might be involved with the same young people. Good links need to be maintained with those with whom youth workers may have to share confidential information, and it is important to be clear about their policies and procedures.

The principle of preserving confidential information gained by youth workers in the course of their work is vital if the young people and communities they work with are to trust them. Yet this principle is not absolute, and there are many occasions, not just when confidentiality will have to be broken, but where confidentiality should never be offered or assumed in the first place. It is these kinds of circumstances that youth workers need to think through in order that they do not feel they are letting young people down by revealing confidential information or taking on intolerable or inappropriate burdens by holding on to young people's confidences. The youth worker is not a counsellor and has a clear role in working for change in society. If some of the private pains of young people are not exposed in the public arena, then some of the changes that need to take place regarding the exploitation, poverty and mistreatment of young people will never be achieved. The youth worker is continually walking a tightrope in trying to balance these concerns. The informal nature of youth work leaves a lot of room for uncertainty and ambiguity. If the youth worker is clear about her role, has thought through some of the issues, considered what exactly is meant by confidentiality, then her job will be easier and young people may feel confused and let down less often.

Acknowledgements

We are grateful to several youth workers for allowing us to use their examples of ethical dilemmas.

Bibliography

Bass, E. and Davis, L. (1988) *The Courage to Heal*, London: Cedar.

Beauchamp, T. and Childress, J. (1994) *Principles of Biomedical Ethics*, Oxford: Oxford University Press.

Biestek, F. (1961) *The Casework Relationship*, London: Allen and Unwin.

Bok, S. (1982) *Secrets: On the Ethics of Concealment and Revelation*, New York, Pantheon.

Bond, T. (1993) *Standards and Ethics for Counselling in Action*, London: Sage.

—— (1995) *Confidentiality about HIV in Multidisciplinary Teams*, Newcastle: Northern and Yorkshire Regional Health Authority.

British Association for Counselling (1993) *Code of Ethics and Practice for Counsellors*, Rugby: BAC.

British Association of Social Workers (1996) *A Code of Ethics for Social Work,* BASW: Birmingham.

Churchill, H. and Honning, T. (1997) 'Student safety matters', *Youth and Policy* 56: 64–8.

City of Newcastle upon Tyne (1996) *Children and Young People's Section Quality Manual*, Newcastle: City of Newcastle upon Tyne Council.

Hill, K. (1995) *The Long Sleep*, London: Virago.

Jeffs, T. and Smith, M. (1996) *Informal Education*, Derby: Education Now Books.

Mander, G. (1997) 'Towards the Millennium: The Counselling Boom', *Counselling* February: 32–5.

Marshall, S (1991) 'Public bodies, private selves' in B. Almond and D. Hill (eds) *Applied Philosophy: Morals and Metaphysics in Contemporary Debate*, London: Routledge.

Nicholls, D. (1995) *Employment Practice and Policies in Youth and Community Work*, Dorset: Russell House Publishing.

North Yorkshire County Council (1989) *Child Abuse Guidelines and Agency Procedures*, Northallerton: North Yorkshire County Council.

Parton, N., Thorpe, D. and Wattam, C. (1997) *Child Protection: Risk and The Moral Order*, London: Macmillan.

Rhodes, M. (1986) *Ethical Dilemmas in Social Work Practice*, Boston MA: Routledge and Kegan Paul.

Sanders, P. (1996) *First Steps in Counselling*, Manchester: PCCS Books.

Shardlow, S. (1995) 'Confidentiality, accountability and the boundaries of client-worker relationships' in R. Hugman and D. Smith (eds) *Ethical Issues in Social Work*, London: Routledge.

Taylor-Browne, J. (1997) 'Obfuscating sexual abuse: 1. The identifications of social problems', *Child Abuse Review* 6: 4–10.

Wilson, S. (1978) *Confidentiaity in Social Work, Issues and Principles*, London: Free Press.

10

RIGHTS-BASED APPROACHES TO WORK WITH YOUNG PEOPLE

David Crimmens and Anna Whalen

Introduction

In this chapter we will look at the values underpinning a rights-based approach to work with young people and explore the contradictions and difficulties in putting these values into practice when working with very marginalised young people. One key plank of social policy is the creation of an inclusive society which clarifies what citizenship means for all stakeholders (Kelly *et al.* 1997). We argue that a rights-based approach can enable practice with young people to be inclusive at a time when young people continue to be crudely categorised by policy makers and the media as either deserving or deviant. This is reflected in current debates about young people's behaviour in schools, in the application of criminal justice legislation and about their position in the labour market. For young people labelled as irresponsible, no hopers or different, the focus of attention is on their deficiencies and lack of responsibility, not on their marginality or the impact of structural inequalities on their individual lives.

We focus on the issues a rights-based practice raises for those working with marginalised young people aged between 11 and 18 years old. We conclude that despite different roles and responsibilities, agencies working with young people could share basic values and apply these in a consistent way. Children's Services Plans provide a mechanism to enable this process to develop. Currently interventions in the lives of very marginalised young people tend towards protection or control in relation to criminal behaviour; little value is placed on their views, aspirations and analyses of their situations. We argue that without an agreed value base between agencies, the impact of any positive work with young people is lessened and the likelihood of social exclusion increased. Marginalised young people rightly view society as treating them unjustly and with disrespect as they continue to have messages about their lack of worth reinforced.

Children, young people, young adults

Fundamental questions about the relationship between people in contemporary society have led to a renewed interest in issues of young people and citizenship (France 1996; West 1996). This interest reflects the complexity of the relationship between independence and dependency in the late twentieth century and wider questions about relationships between individuals and the state reflected in notions of citizenship (Oliver 1994). Political rights define the formal relationship between adults and the state reflected in the right to vote. Young people legally acquire adult status on their eighteenth birthday. Before this landmark young people are defined as children in UK domestic legislation such as the Children Act 1989 and in international agreements such as the UN Convention on the Rights of the Child (CRC). The status of a child is characterised legally as dependent, but this simple dichotomy masks a growing complexity in the real world. This is particularly the case when distinctions between adults and children are further differentiated to include young people.

The term 'young people' is conventionally used to include some of those who are legally defined as children. It also includes those who are formally adult in the age group 18–25 years. Coles (1995: 89) argues that any discussion on citizenship, rights and responsibilities should see young people, or youth, as a category separate from children, as:

> a state of relative semi-independency and autonomy during which [they] go through a series of staged progressions to the independence of adulthood.

There is an ongoing debate about the position of young people in society and their access to resources. Age is not the only category which differentiates people: class, gender, ethnicity, ability and sexual orientation also have a profound impact on the opportunity structure and access to resources which are needed to participate actively in contemporary society. A traditional assumption that adult status defines full citizenship conferring independence and autonomy is a myth for growing sections of the population who remain dependent on their families and the state. While their eighteenth birthday marks a formal transition to full enfranchisement with the right to vote, this political status is not matched by equivalent economic and social independence for many young people. Social rights, in relation to access to welfare irrespective of the individual's location in the labour market, could provide young people with the independence and autonomy implied by adult status (Coote 1992; Twine 1994; Dean 1996).

Jones (1995) emphasises the importance of economic independence, achieved largely through paid employment, as the key which unlocks access to a range of other rights. This follows the basic foundations of Marshall's (1950) theories of citizenship which are predicated on assumptions about full employment and the primacy of the male breadwinner. These assumptions, while relevant at the time when these ideas were developed, do not take account of structural changes in the labour market which have resulted in the long-term unemployment of significant populations of young people.

Coles criticises Marshall for failing fully to explore how different status groups in society can be granted different kinds of citizenship. He suggests that this leaves the bulk of the population who are neither adult nor male, and those without paid employment, with a problematic status. For citizenship to have any meaning in defining rights and entitlements:

> it must be capable...not only of specifying universal rights but must also be capable of addressing the different rights of different categories of citizen who live in different social, economic and material conditions.
>
> (Coles 1995: 82)

It has always been problematic to know at what point to stop referring to children as such and to start using the term 'young people'. This reflects a general confusion about the place of children and young people in society. In the absence of clear demarcation lines, we will use the term young people, though much of what we discuss is applicable to those who continue to be defined legally as children. Jones (1996) suggests that original conceptions of linear transitions from childhood to adulthood have been superseded by extended periods of transition which leave many young people with, at best, an uncertain status. Clear boundaries between childhood and adulthood are blurred to the extent that many young people are unable to exercise their rights and responsibilities as citizens due to lack of access to resources and opportunity structures. Consequently, these young people, who may have crossed the traditional boundary into formal legal adulthood, retain elements of dependency and vulnerability. This may result in their position being more comparable to that of children than that of adults.

Citizenship and rights

The need to develop and promote citizenship and rights in Britain is gaining momentum in national and local politics. This is reflected in legislation on human rights, lobbying for a statutory independent Office of Children's Rights Commissioner (Hodgkin and Newell 1996) comparable to the Ombudsman for children already constituted in a number of European countries, discussions on stake-holding in society (Hutton 1995), and the development of consultation mechanisms in local authorities such as youth councils (Willow 1997).

In relation to children and young people under eighteen, citizenship status and rights for children and young people are conventionally contested on the basis that they are not able or responsible enough to make decisions, and there are others much better positioned to make decisions on their behalf. Flekkoy and Kaufmann (1997) make the point that young people need to learn the skills and aptitudes of effective participation in democratic processes in order to be effective citizens. Hart (1992) and Knuttson (1996) argue that young people need to be more involved in their communities and civic society, not just to gain skills and experience for the future, but because their contribution is relevant and valuable to society now. For those young people who are treated as problems, involvement in their communities can shape their perceptions of society and their place within it, as well as provide policy makers and planners with valuable insights into needs-led services and effective use of resources. Youth councils and forums are not likely to be the route by which very marginalised young people are consulted. Imaginative mechanisms to promote their claims to citizenship and the value of their contributions need to be explored. Without a commitment to engagement and participation of marginal young people they will continue to be perceived only as a problem.

Universal rights, applied without reference to inequality and tied up with notions of responsibility, will favour those who are middle and upper class, white, male, economically active, heterosexual and not disabled. We argue against a universal, blanket approach to rights, on the basis that everyone might have rights but accessing them is dependent on individuals' and groups' positions of power in society. Extended dependency for some groups of young people results in them retaining many of the characteristics and vulnerabilities of younger age groups. They continue to suffer discrimination on the basis of their class, ethnicity, gender, ability and sexuality, as well as their age. Accepting that young people have specific rights reduces their dependence on adults to provide, protect and speak for them and hence their individual and collective vulnerability is lessened.

Rights and citizenship for all young people are equally important for the wider community in furthering the development of democracy. The situations of disadvantaged young people need to be addressed in order to reduce existing inequalities and create a more inclusive civic society. We need to recognise that young people have entitlements or rights because they are young people, and that adults have a responsibility for ensuring that they are able to access these rights. Active commitment to practices which carry out these responsibilities reflects a set of values which recognise young people as active participants rather than passive consumers (Baker 1996).

Marginalised and socially excluded young people

In most major cities in Britain there are young people who have effectively been pushed out on to the edges or margins of society, where they are wholly or partially excluded from participating in the communities in which they live. These young people have been called 'street children' (Wynn-Jones 1997; Frost 1997), 'runaways' (Stein et al. 1994), and 'superpredators' (Grey 1997). However, no label rests easily or reflects accurately their very different situations. They adapt to their adverse circumstances by adopting lifestyles which may place them at risk. These risks include drug use, violent and petty crime (both as victim and perpetrator), prostitution, sleeping in derelict buildings, on the street or in flats occupied by other young people or adults who are also leading similar lifestyles. Other risks, which may be less obvious are those of neglect and the health problems related to this lifestyle – diet, hygiene, exposure to diseases found within the street community, hypothermia and mental

Quantifying is problematic: numbers are fluid, situa-
example, many young people who run away return
days. Young people may live at home, but to all
ses lead a street lifestyle. Many are on the periphery
ers are at risk, there are difficulties at home and
1 the home and the peer group. The trigger factors
...to such a lifestyle are various, including family breakdown, abuse
at home, parents with drug or mental health problems, exclusion or
non-attendance at school, or being looked after by a local authority.
There is no single profile of a young person at risk – gender, age,
class, ethnicity, sexuality, disability and family circumstances all
determine differences. Although not an homogeneous group, they
do share the common experiences of youth and their marginality
from society.

It is not unusual for any young people in this age group to avoid
contact with adults who represent some kind of authority to them,
whether they are teachers, social workers, education welfare officers
or youth workers. What is different about young people who are at
risk is they are often so dislocated from their families and communities that they cannot be made to see anyone they do not want to.
They effectively live outside the sphere of adult authority and
control, but equally outside access to systems of help and support.
They slip through safety nets which are restricted by the limitations
of statutory responses. Many say they want to be left alone, that
they can look after themselves and have survival tactics to do just
that. Homeless under-16 year olds are not able to get into hostels or
claim any benefit, so without the support of a family or social
services department, survival is about stealing, begging, or selling
sex or drugs. But often those who have been adamant that they do
not want to make changes reach a point of desperation and seek
help. The success of this is varied. Young people at risk do not fit
easily into conventional service provision.

The agencies providing or coordinating services for young people
at risk have to manage a tension in practice which arises from the
duties placed upon them to protect young people under the
Children Act 1989. It is ironic in this context that the more the state
attempts to intervene to protect young people at risk, the more
many young people actively avoid such interventions and become
more at risk in the process. The challenge for practitioners working
with highly marginalised young people is how to work with the
contradictions involved in optimising autonomy for young people
enabling them to maintain control over their own lives, while at the

same time confronting the consequences of the abuse and exploitation which they face.

A rights-based approach

The practice issues raised are informed by the UN Convention on the Rights of the Child (CRC), a universally recognised document. This lays down basic rights for young people up to the age of eighteen all over the world. The Convention can be broadly divided into three sections – protection rights, provision rights and political rights. The Convention is not law, but sets standards for the way children and young people are to be treated.

The principles underpinning the Children Act 1989 coincide at many points with the CRC; for example: treating all young people as individuals; parental responsibility towards (rather than rights over) young people; decisions made in the best interests of each young person; and ascertaining their wishes and feelings when making decisions which affect them. A crucial element of this legislation is about young people having rights themselves, such as the right to be consulted and to make complaints, leaving adults with duties towards, rather than rights over, them as young people.

A rights-based approach is not simply knowing what young people are legally entitled to. Knowledge of rights can be translated into values which underpin work with young people. Newell (1991) reminds us that a commitment to these values starts with our own daily relationships with the young people we work and live with. This is reinforced by others, such as Thompson (1993), who emphasise the importance of addressing the powerlessness of young people at the level of individual practice as well as at institutional and structural levels. The values in practice proposed here are essential to working with young people in a consistent, rights-focused way:

- Treating all young people as individuals with dignity and respect: the basis of the Children Act (1989) and the United Nations Convention is non-discrimination.
- Listening carefully to what young people have to say and taking their views seriously: without this a rights approach is meaningless.
- Communicating all information, including that on rights, in an accessible, young-person-friendly way: without information young people do not know what their rights are and cannot make informed contributions in decision-making.

- Involving young people in decisions that may affect their lives and actively seeking opportunities to do this on an individual and collective basis, using both adult and self-advocacy.

Participation in decision-making is one way in which young people can take more control in their lives and experience the sense of power which emerges from the ensuing autonomy. Treseder (1997) emphasises that a key element of empowerment must be about the involvement of young people, their active participation in the development of policies and practices which affect the services that are directed at young people. Enabling young people to participate in this way requires significant changes in culture and style of organisations delivering services. It also requires changes in attitudes on the part of people working in those organisations to ensure that commitments to participation are translated from rhetoric into the realities of practice. Involving young people who are experiencing chaos in their daily lives can be difficult. They have different priorities and processes of empowerment are slow.

All of the above values mean being open and honest about what is going on, including clarifying boundaries and power and authority roles, being up-front about issues such as confidentiality and child protection procedures, acknowledging any mistakes made, and learning from young people's contributions. Adults working with young people have different employers, policies, resources, responsibilities and time commitments, but a shared rights-based approach is not radical or unrealistic. Individuals working in social work, the police, education and youth work follow these principles all the time, but there is a lack of consistency across agencies. It is about treating young people in the same way we expect to be treated ourselves, and how we would expect our own children to be treated.

Dilemmas of intervention

Working with very disadvantaged young people is often not just about how one agency or staff group work, but how a range of agencies work together, their different roles and responsibilities and how values and the practice undertaken by agencies fit together to provide support and opportunities for young people. There are two systems of intervention that young people at risk are likely to encounter: child protection and criminal justice systems. Both demonstrate in very different ways the difficulties of working with young people at risk and the potential for conflict and disagreement between agencies about ethical practice. Child protection, more than any other system which relates to the needs of young people, illustrates the dilemmas for contemporary practice with young people. There is an expectation that the state will intervene to protect vulnerable people from abuse and exploitation. Yet state intervention is provided in ways which compromise the potential of young people to be self-determining by adopting a paternalistic approach to service delivery. One contradiction is that young people become less entitled to state protection as they get older, with a legal cut-off for most young people at the point of achieving adult status.

Child protection

Local authorities have a statutory duty to protect children and young people who are experiencing or are likely to experience significant harm. Concerns about young people at risk may be raised due to a combination of any of the following: neglect, sexual or physical abuse, being missing for long periods of time, drug use or sexual exploitation. Recent research (HMSO 1995) acknowledges that child protection has come to dominate social work with children and their families in the last fifteen years at the expense of prevention and support services. The considerations in intervention can be based on a number of factors:

- the likelihood of a young person experiencing significant harm – the basis for compulsory state intervention in protecting young people;
- questions of whether this significant harm is posed by an external threat or a lifestyle 'choice';
- official perceptions of the level of risk;
- the young person's perception of the risk;
- the young person's previous experience of child protection interventions;
- the young person's relationship with their family;
- resources available;
- perceptions of short and long term outcomes.

Extreme situations can lead to extreme responses from statutory agencies. If a young person already has a history of running away from a children's home or foster carer, placement in an out-of-authority children's home or a secure children's home may be considered as the only way to protect a young person. The right to participate is often overlooked in the face of imperatives to protect, in spite of requirements under the Children Act 1989 to ascertain young people's wishes and feelings about their situations. Why is it so difficult to involve young people at risk in decision-making about their welfare and protection? Grimshaw and Sinclair (1997) highlight the difficulties of effectively involving young people in decision-making when there is no immediate crisis. It is therefore less surprising that practitioners experience difficulty enabling young people to participate when they are subject to child protection procedures.

There is no prevailing culture within child protection processes of listening to young people, in spite of the underlying principles of the legislation, except in court proceedings (Parton 1996). Time to talk is not given a priority unless evidence is required for the purposes of prosecution. Adults decide what constitutes a crisis: a young person's understanding and concerns may be very different. Young people defined as being at risk see themselves as survivors and may not feel that they need protection. Failure actively to enable them to participate in the process can increase their feelings of alienation and polarise their position relative to the social workers. Many of these young people are already well known to social services departments and have acquired reputations as impossible to work with, and so little effort is put into communicating with them about their right to be involved in the decision-making process. This reinforces what they feel about adults as untrustworthy and controlling. This produces a no-win situation for both the young person and the workers. Their lack of involvement or consultation can result in young people going underground to avoid intervention, potentially increasing the risks they already face.

As a result of their detachment from child protection decision-making, actions can appear arbitrary to young people. For example, two young people can be living the same kind of life: one is placed on the Child Protection Register, the other has no social worker allocated; one may go to a secure children's home, the other to foster carers. Decisions seem beyond the control of young people. The level of discretion available to social workers is viewed by young people as inconsistent and confusing, and this is one of the reasons why they avoid contact – they do not know what might happen.

Placing young people at risk in children's homes or foster families in order to protect them is often not effective in the long term in the absence of the young person's commitment to the placement. It is a safe short-term solution for local authorities that lack the resources and time to think about a more creative response. This is a difficult point to sustain when confronted with the pressure arising from the belief that a particular intervention is in the best interests of the young person and the lack of an obvious alternative. There is little research about what young people at risk perceive as their best interests and solutions to the problems that they define. Yet, in a child protection situation, they should be the major stakeholders. Some young people have a very different sense of the world, their place in it and what the rules are. They appear to have taken Thatcherite principles of individualism and personal responsibility to the extreme: they do not want any form of state intervention in their lives. This may be a rational response to their perception of reality. Fox-Harding (1996) suggests that empowerment may have been redefined to mean that people are increasingly having to rely on their own resources as state services are withdrawn.

Failure to take account of the very different perceptions young people have about their lives results in continuing to treat them as passive victims, which is not how they perceive themselves. There are other pragmatic reasons why involving young people at risk is essential to their long-term welfare. These are that:

- no involvement reinforces what they already believe about adults not listening and being untrustworthy;
- the lack of negotiation may mean the intervention is experienced as a punishment rather than protection;
- should a young person run away again they may be more at risk through becoming more difficult to make contact with.

A rights-based approach may involve higher levels of risk-taking to optimise young people's involvement in decision-making processes in order to reduce their sense of exclusion. There is a tension between this approach and the need to offer effective protection. Benign neglect could be one consequence if commitments to increasing participation degenerate into laissez-faire practices. A negotiated pathway is needed between the wishes and feelings of the young person and statutory requirements to ensure that the process and outcomes of decision-making are experienced as being in the young person's best interests. Increasing the active involvement of young people in risk situations is likely to lessen their sense of exclusion from society.

Law and order

In the arena of youth anti-social and criminal behaviour, policy and public anxiety is focused currently on young boys. Consultation documents such as 'Tackling Youth Crime' (Home Office 1997a) and the subsequent White Paper (Home Office 1997b) emphasise an official commitment to holding young people accountable for their behaviour in a context which defines young people as the 10–17-year-old age group. Driven by powerful and threatening images like 'rat boy' and the killers of Jamie Bulger, the 'new barbarians' (Field 1996) effectively produce another moral panic about the danger and threat to social order of young boys. The Criminal Justice and Public Order Act (1993) responded to fears about drug taking and the lawlessness of New Age Travellers by criminalising raves and other illegal gatherings at the other end of the age group. Rising levels of custodial sentences reflect a more traditional strategy of using the prison system to maintain social discipline among young people.

Abolition of the ancient common law of *'doli incapax'* suggests that, from ten years old, young people are going to be expected to take full responsibility for their own behaviour as if they were adults. This change is consistent with trends which emphasise the responsibilities of young people. Central to current strategies is a reinforcement of parental responsibilities starting with pushing financial responsibility for 16–18 year olds back into the family as part of a process of withdrawing direct state support for young people.

What happens to those young people who are unable to depend on their families for financial support and accommodation? In the absence of state support they can be dependent on services in the voluntary sector. They are also likely to be increasingly subject to disciplinary measures designed to force them to take more responsibility for themselves using welfare-to-work to ensure their readiness for work should the opportunities arise in the labour market. In the meantime, claiming income support through complex procedures involved in the Job Seekers Allowance may be actively avoided by young people at risk. Recent forms of income generation for young people such as squeegee merchants and begging are likely to be criminalised by zero tolerance policing.

Young people at risk are likely to be involved in anti-social activity, some of which will be criminal in order to survive, to feed a drug habit, to have some excitement and/or to fit in with their peers. Their civil rights are explicitly codified in the criminal justice system and some potential for vulnerability is recognised in the Police and Criminal Evidence Act. However there is less tolerance in the current climate towards their anti-social behaviour and little concern about the structural reasons which marginalise and socially exclude. Emphasis on conformity and control results in punishment for those who are seen to be unable to take appropriate responsibility for themselves.

One way forward

A rights-based approach is one way forward for practice. Tension exists in practice which aims to help young people get what they should be entitled to. The clamour for changing their behaviour and getting them to take responsibility for themselves is contradicted when intervention is tried as a means of protection and young people experience this as taking away their responsibility. Young people at risk go to great lengths to avoid such help as a statement about their need to control something in their lives. In an era of increasing targeting of state resources and declining charitable funding without strings attached, working with young people who are unwilling to accept the price tags to any intervention may become increasingly difficult.

A rights-based approach needs to build on local and national policy. It needs to build on the responsibilities which signature of international agreements such as the CRC require. Since 31 March 1997, each local authority has a mandatory duty to produce an annual Children's Services Plan. The aim of this plan is to deliver better services to children and young people 'in need' (a term which is explicitly defined in Section 17 of the Children Act 1989) by increased planning, coordination, identification of gaps and duplication, priority setting and review. In order to do this effectively, local authorities are obliged to involve statutory and voluntary agencies in the planning and reviewing processes. Most importantly in this context, local authorities are required to consult with service users, young people and their parents about the plans.

Currently, the profile of Children's Services Plans is minimal. Many agencies who work with young people are unaware of their potential. On the surface it does not sound very exciting, but the duty placed upon the local authority to consult and involve gives agencies which are traditionally marginalised in formal decision-making processes, such as small voluntary organisations and youth services, an opportunity to influence the development of local services for young people in need. The Department for Education and Employment, Department of Health, the Home Office and the National Health Service Executive have issued guidance which is not prescriptive, but encourages local authorities to broaden the Children Act definition of 'in need' if this is deemed appropriate. Consequently, the needs of marginalised young people who do not fit prescriptive criteria may be recognised and addressed if consultation processes permit.

More significantly for those who are committed to promoting a rights approach, every Children's Services Plan clearly identifies the CRC as a set of underlying principles when planning services for young people. Practitioners with a philosophy and practice of listening to and involving young people can legitimately expect to be taken seriously. Young people must be involved and those with responsibility for drawing up the plans are likely to be looking for creative good practice in this area. There remains an unknown potential for young people to be involved in policy and practice development in agencies which have traditionally paid lip service to participation issues. Sutton (1995) believes that this potential could be used to raise young people's issues higher in public and political agendas, contributing to a national debate on the status of young people with rights and responsibilities of their own.

Conclusions

We have examined some of the issues involved in practice with marginalised and excluded young people. We have explored some of the tensions and contradictions involved in working within a legal framework which can deprive young people of their right to express their own views in situations where adults decide that, in their best interests, they need protection. The right to be protected legally ends, with few exceptions, at the formal acquisition of adulthood. Significant numbers of young adults, who may have formally achieved adult status, do not have access to the economic and social resources to secure their autonomy and independence. Young people aged 16–18 years may have 'zero status', but at least they retain the entitlements of domestic legislation and the CRC.

Listening to those with least power is essential in order to reduce their social exclusion. Paradoxically, the most marginalised are, by definition, the most difficult to engage with, due to their structural disadvantages and the resulting pathologising of their individual circumstances. Marginalised young people do not have many positive experiences to draw on from their involvement with families, the community or the state and may have very low expectations as a consequence. Responsibility for creating the opportunities for their inclusion rests with adults in state and voluntary agencies who have the power and access to resources. Commitment to their rights provides an alternative to continuing to see such young people as undeserving or deviant. As the transitions to adulthood continue to be extended, concerted action by progressive practitioners is required to ensure that a generation of the more disadvantaged groups of young people is not lost to the prison or the street. There is a tension between protection, control and ensuring that young people are able to participate in society in ways in which they are able to express their own views and opinions. We are inclined to agree with Beatrix Campbell (1997) who says that ultimately these debates are more about what it means to be an adult than the rights of children and young people. The recognition that all young people are entitled to access to resources enabling them to attain a lifestyle that is recognised as civilised and prepares them for their roles as adults must therefore constitute a moral purpose which contributes towards a mutual understanding of what will constitute the future society of the twenty-first century.

Bibliography

Baker, J. (1996) *The Fourth Partner: Participant or Consumer?* Leicester: Youth Work Press.

Campbell, B. (1997) 'Consider the children', *Community Care* 9–16 January.

Coles, B. (1995) *Youth and Social Policy: Youth Citizenship and Young Careers*, London: UCL Press.

Coote, A. (ed.) (1992) *The Welfare of Citizens: Developing New Social Rights*, London: IPPR/Rivers Oram Press.

Dean, H. (1996) *Welfare Law and Citizenship*, Hemel Hempstead: Prentice Hall/Harvester Wheatsheaf.

Field, F. (1996) 'How we can tame the new barbarians', *Daily Mail* 3 December.

Flekkoy, M. and Kaufman, N. (1997) *Rights and Responsibilities in Family and Society*, London: Jessica Kingsley.

Fox-Harding, L. (1996) 'Recent developments in "children's rights": liberation for whom?' *Child and Family Social Work* 1: 141–50.

France, A. (1996) 'Youth and citizenship in the 1990's', *Youth and Policy* 53: 28–43.

Frost, M. (1997) 'They call this childhood?' *Independent on Sunday* 8 June.

Grey, S. (1997) 'Invasion of the superpredators,' *Sunday Times* 16 February.

Grimshaw, R. and Sinclair, R. (1997) *Planning to Care: Regulation, Procedure and Practice under the Children Act 1989*, London: National Children's Bureau.

Hart, R. (1992) *Children's Participation: From Tokenism to Citizenship*, Innocenti Essays 4, Florence: Unicef International Child Development Centre.

HMSO (1995) *Child Protection: Messages from Research*, London: HMSO.

Hodgkin, R. and Newell, P. (1996) *Effective Government Structures for Children*, report of a Gulbenkian Foundation Inquiry, London: Calouste Gulbenkian Foundation.

Home Office (1997a) *Tackling Youth Crime: A Consultation Paper*, London: HMSO.

—— (1997b) *No More Excuses: A New Approach to Tackling Youth Crime in England and Wales*, White Paper, 27 November, London: HMSO.

Hutton, W. (1995) *The State We're In*, London: Jonathan Cape.

Jenkins, P. (1993) *Children's Rights: A Participative Exercise for Learning about Children's Rights in England and Wales*, Harlow: Longman.

Jones, G. (1995): *Deferred Citizenship: A Coherent Policy of Exclusion*, Occasional Paper no. 3, Leicester: National Youth Agency.

—— (1996) 'Deferred citizenship', *Young People Now* March 1996.

Kelly, G., Kelly D. and Gamble, A. (1997) *Stakeholder Capitalism*, London: Macmillan.

Knutsson, K. (1996) 'A new vision of childhood', in *The Child as Citizen*, Strasbourg: Council of Europe Publishing.

Marshall, T. H. (1950) *Citizenship and Social Class and other Essays*, Cambridge: Cambridge University Press.

Newell, P. (1991) *The UN Convention and Children's Rights in the UK*, London: National Children's Bureau.

Oliver, D. (1994) 'What is happening to the relationship between the individual and the state?', in D. Oliver and J. Jowell *The Changing Constitution*, Oxford: Clarendon Press.

Parton, N. (1996) 'The new politics of child protection', in S. Wagg and J. Pilcher (eds) *Thatcher's Children: Childhood and Society in the 1980s and 1990s*, London: Falmer Press.

Stein, M., Rees, G. and Frost, N. (1994) *Running the Risk: Young People on the Streets of Britain Today*, London: Children's Society.

Sutton, P. (1995) *Crossing the Boundaries: A Discussion of Children's Services Plans*, London: National Children's Bureau.

Thompson, N. (1993) *Anti-Discriminatory Practice*, Basingstoke: Macmillan.

Treseder, P. (1997) *Empowering Children and Young People: A training manual*, London: Save the Children.

Twine, F. (1994) *Citizenship and Social Rights. The Interdependence of Self and Society*, London: Sage.

West, A. (1996) 'Citizenship, children and young people', *Youth and Policy* 55: 69–74.

Willow, C. (1997) *Hear! Hear! Promoting Children and Young People's Democratic Participation in Local Government*, London: Local Government Information Unit.

Wynn-Jones, R. (1997) 'Children sleeping on the street. Rio? No Britain tonight', *Independent on Sunday*, 8 June.

11

YOUNG PEOPLE AS RESEARCHERS

Ethical issues in participatory research

Andy West

Introduction

Young people are the focus of much research. An increasing number of journals are devoted to their lives, supported and partly driven by the continued revision of current media forms of youth as folk devils, ensuring a steady stream of attention. Much of this research is by adults investigating young people as 'other'. Such investigation is political, and a broad analogy can be drawn with the European mapping of other lands as part of the process of exercising control, colonising and trade through a knowledge of local society.

This chapter will explore an approach to research based on values and methods emphasised in youth work – empowerment, participation and informal education – within a framework of young people's rights: participatory research *by* rather than *on* young people. Good participatory research in its content and findings is at least of equal value to that produced from traditional methods, but the tensions between the empowerment of young people and conventional research validity produce a set of processual dilemmas that illustrate the social relationship and status of adults and young people, and are indicative of some general ethical problems in good youth work practice.

Youth workers and research

Youth workers' involvement in research has mostly been as gate-keepers, rather than investigating the lives of the young people with whom they work. Similarly with social work: 'research always seemed to be something that other professionals and social workers in academia engaged in but not something that social workers in practice had much to do with' (Gleed 1996: 13). However, social work and health professionals are increasingly interested in developing research as a means of empowering themselves as practitioners. This research is often based on values of acknowledging individual integrity and knowledge, rights to be heard, collective action and challenging oppression (Everitt et al.1992: 37–8; Everitt and Gibson 1994; Hart and Bond 1995; Fook 1996). Youth work practice is beginning to change, evidenced by articles in the journal *Youth and Policy*, and a number of recent participatory projects (for example, Hackett et al. 1996; Munday 1996; Nevison 1997; Waldman and Hague 1996; West et al. 1995). However, many youth workers who do research transfer to the academy, or are already teaching. But research should be as much of a concern for youth workers as other aspects of social policy which shape and constrain young people's lives.

Traditional social research has essentially been 'us and them', outsiders and insiders, with one group having a set of questions about another. The purpose of the research may vary, from gaining a qualification and career to reinforcing policy making. Some adults (undergraduate or postgraduate students) are not much older than the youth they are researching; the research divide is not just about adults and young people, but socio-economic position and education. Researchers are trained in methodology so their work stands up to the scrutiny of professional peers; it immediately becomes distant from the people who are the subjects of the study.

Critiques of traditional research have abounded for some time, particularly around notions of subject–object separation, the idea of value-free research and of objective reality (Fook 1996: 189–99). The roles and relationships of the researcher and researched have been questioned, stimulated by feminist perspectives (Stanley 1990). Critiques of development research in the South[1] indicated the failure of outsiders coming into research. New techniques of research were devised, focused on a participatory relationship with local people as teachers and outside researchers as learners (Chambers 1994; Cornwall and Jewkes 1995). The work was rapid[2] and qualitative, drawing on anthropological methods such as participant observation, mixed with innovative techniques, such as creating social maps using materials to hand.

Fundamental concerns in this participatory research paradigm include people's rights of ownership over the research, their lives and ideas, and the relationship between local people, outsiders and institutions. These concerns pose ethical questions around professional interventions and the participation of 'client' groups. Research as an intervention raises issues which contribute to general problems and concerns of ethical practice. In terms of youth work and research, the relations of power are threefold: first, power of the adult (youth worker) over young people; second, power of the researcher over the researched; and third, power of professional over client group. These relationships are explored below through the example of young people's research on leaving care.

Participatory research

Participatory research is difficult to define because of the continuum of participation involved, sometimes seen as a ladder (Hart 1992) or wheel (Treseder 1997) offering degrees of participation and power sharing. For young people involved in research it would run from being researched, to asking questions on behalf of adults, through to establishing research content and purpose. A simple continuum line is insufficient, since young people could be involved to different degrees in various aspects of the research process: in analysis, writing up, designing outputs and questions.

Writers and practitioners use terminology involving participation and research in many different ways. It is important to consider the extent and nature of participation involved, the underlying philosophy and the purpose of the research.[3] Everitt et al. (1992: 14) suggest that 'in participatory research, the subjects of the research are involved in the research process', and 'the essential relationship between the research process and the research task is addressed through its primary method, dialogue. Data are created through discussions amongst all participants in the process of service delivery'. 'Participatory Action Research' is a term widely used, emphasising that people involved in the research are not to be treated as passive subjects and challenging the elitist model of professional researchers doing applied research (Whyte 1991). A distinction often made about 'participative research' is that it concerns 'research with people rather than research on people' (Reason 1994: 1). The terms participative and participatory are held by some to have different meanings, while others use them synonymously.

Here, participatory research is taken to mean a joint process of inquiry, but one led by the community group: not on, nor with, but *by* the group. That is, research led and conducted by young people and supported by adults, as distinct from young people participating in adult's research and from peer research. Indeed the term 'peer research' is a misnomer, rather suggesting that young people awake one day and decide to do research. Youth peer research projects are usually initiated, supported and resourced by adults, and for a particular purpose. The rationale may be to develop young people's skills and confidence through a participatory piece of work, or it may be that peers conducting interviews, analysis, and so on, is seen as a specially useful method of doing the work, acquiring data and insight (West 1997).

Part of the joint inquiry process is the empowerment of the community group. But if one of the aims of participatory research is empowerment, it is important to ask who or what is the research for, and who makes the decision about purpose? The answer might take three possible forms. First, the research may be undertaken for an outside agency using young people as researchers because of benefits of access to other young people, quality of data gathered, etc. – essentially employing young people. Second, the research may aim primarily to offer experience and opportunity – an emphasis on young people's learning and development. Third, the research may be a mixture of the two, both the agency and young people deciding purpose, as happened in the leaving care research described below, enabling and supporting young people to give voice to their needs and circumstances, and providing information and group advocacy based on knowledge and experience. The third approach might seem to offer the best of the other two, but involves greater complexities in decision-making.

Research for the outside agency, using young people as researchers, means that decisions are made by that agency; professional researchers can retain control through the research design, with young people's input limited in practice. Research by and for young people, largely as an exercise in their participation, with them making decisions, including design, gives them control and may not utilise any professional input. In mixing the two forms, the emphasis of participation varies throughout the process: for example, young people making decisions, but asking for information and advice, and deciding whether to use it or not.

These underlying relationships express themselves in various ways throughout and after a research project is completed. At the heart of the participatory research process is the fact that power in general lies with adults, the opportunity for young people to participate is granted by adults, and may be withheld by them even unintentionally. Undertaking any participatory project requires that youth workers and other adults involved continually reflect upon what they are doing, and how it fits with their aims and intentions. Participatory research throws these points of process into the spotlight. The importance of undertaking ethical research has been discussed (Homan 1991) and emphasised by professional institutions (BSA n.d.). Ethical issues such as informed consent and ownership are multiplied in participatory research led and conducted by young people where the roles of researcher and researched become blurred. A major task is to manage the tensions to ensure the research is empowering, valid and credible.

Participation and youth work

Key elements linking youth work and participatory research are the process itself, an aspect of informal education and learning: the notion of 'starting where young people are' (beginning from their perspective), and the value of empowerment. A beginning point with participatory research is that young people want to do it, that the research is purposeful and has meaning to them, just as young people voluntarily engage in youth work activities.

Participation has been an aspect of youth work for many years (see Smith 1988), and is a vital element in informal education. Manuals have been produced for participatory practice (for example, Gordon n.d.; Joyce n.d.), and government reports have emphasised participation (HMSO 1960, 1982). Participation was seen as a means of achieving young people's personal development and social education. Throughout the 1980s participation (for example, involvement in running a centre) was seen as integral to youth work practice (Lacey 1987). The struggle to become democratic in work with young people, while maintaining a value base of, for example, anti-sexist work (Rosseter 1987), showed that the focus of participation was not merely young people engaging in activities, but involved their decision-making.

The contested term 'social education' (Smith 1988) has been popular among many youth workers as a description and rationale of their practice. The term had the notion of participation at its core (Smith 1980), including young people as users of clubs, involved in organising activities, and making decisions from budgetary matters to appointing staff. Smith (1988) highlighted problems with the imprecise use of 'social education'. In a similar fashion, the terms participation/participatory have become value-laden and practice obscured by a lack of critical attention (West 1996b). The many facets of participatory research with young people show that it too risks being superficially understood, failing to be fully developed and so properly conferring potential benefits of empowerment and increasing knowledge. Because youth work has not been at the forefront of research, it has largely ignored participation in research.

Young people's research on leaving care

Throughout the 1980s the problems faced by young people leaving the care[4] of the local authority became exacerbated by diminishing welfare provision for young people in general at a time of severe and increasing unemployment and homelessness, and decreasing opportunity. Many agencies established projects to work with children in care and young people who had left care. In 1994 funding became available for the England programme of Save the Children Fund (SCF) to research issues of leaving care.[5] It was decided that the research would be participatory – that it would be done by young people themselves. This was an important decision. The issue of leaving care had been researched (for example, Stein and Carey 1986; Garnett 1992) with other work ongoing (Biehal *et al.* 1995). Some thought further work unnecessary, the problem being less a lack of research and more a lack of action by government and local authorities. The issue of research recommendations being largely ignored is not uncommon. The difficulties faced by young people who had recently left care still existed, and the purpose of the project was for their voice to be heard through their own research.

A small steering group of adults was established, and a framework for the research decided. Five SCF projects across England, in Bolton, Kirklees, Leeds, London and Oxford[6] became involved. Each project recruited two young people who had recently left care – a total of ten (three young men and seven young women), most aged 16–18 years. The framework was five residential meetings (each of two or three days), with the young people working from their SCF project bases in between. The residential meetings were the main point of decision-making for the young researchers: these were the only occasions all ten could meet together because of the distances involved. The fieldwork was conducted in their home localities, with the SCF projects providing office space, resources, and, most importantly, support from staff. Although young people were the driving force in the project, a number of adult staff were engaged, providing support for the young researchers at home and on the residentials, facilitating the development of the work, writing it up, publication, media work and follow-up work with central and local government. Two SCF youth workers provided support at residentials (one also acted as administrator). An adult facilitator was used at the residentials, and an adult researcher acted as facilitator and the focal point for developing the research with the young people, seeing it through to publication and liaising with funders, steering group and across SCF departments. The research fell into the six stages described below.

Establishing the research

The researchers shared their experience. Their knowledge of leaving care provided the expertise on which the research was based. The process of sharing demonstrated common experiences and issues across England. They decided the purpose and format of research. The young people wanted the issues and experience of leaving care to be communicated to the public, and were concerned that the findings should not be left on the shelf.

Setting the framework and method

The researchers decided on a semi-structured interview schedule, open to the interviewees, which could be completed by interviewer or interviewee. They decided to interview young people who had recently left care, or were just in process of leaving (their delicate distinction), and staff who worked with young people who were leaving and had left care. Their aim was to complete 100 interviews with young people and 50 with staff. Each young researcher took responsibility to complete between 12 and 15 interviews. From the sharing of knowledge and experience, a framework of key issues emerged, used as the basis for the interview schedules. Two long semi-structured interview schedules were compiled and piloted by the young people – one for young care leavers and one for staff.

Doing the work

Prior to compiling the schedule, before undertaking fieldwork, and in 'debriefing' sessions, the young researchers practised developing questions and interview techniques through experiential learning.

They finally completed a total of 80 interviews with young people and 22 with staff (not all were done in time for the final report, based on 77 young care leavers and 21 staff). They were supported by staff throughout this process.

Developing a report

Key points on the qualitative analysis were developed by the young researchers at the residentials. Recommendations were developed in skeleton over three residentials and worked up in detail at the last, including a calculation of the minimum leaving care grant required. The conclusion to the report was written in outline as a group at the final residential, and a title created and agreed. The final report was written up by an adult, using an agreed framework and the analysis and work of the young researchers. The bulk of the draft was approved at the last residential, and the final draft afterwards, by post.

Launch and dissemination

The launch format was agreed between the young people and the SCF press office, who also offered training in working with journalists. The published research, a report, separate summary and video were presented to an all-party group of MPs at a London press conference by three young researchers. Other researchers launched the work from their SCF project bases. Afterwards, many interviewees and other young people from the local projects continued making presentations and showing the video to local authorities and other groups. Some researchers and other care leavers attended a private members' debate on leaving care, which quoted extensively from their work. During the debate the minister invited young care leavers to meet him to discuss the issues: one of the young researchers attended.

Findings

The findings from care leavers focused on ten issues: income, housing, health, support, work, education, public attitude, police, social life, preparation for leaving care. In short, care-leaver's experiences included: low or no income, poor or no housing, health problems, inadequate or no support, few employment opportunities, limited educational experiences, being condemned or patronised by the public, being troubled by the police, poor social life and limited preparation for leaving care. All the issues are interlinked, but the first four on this list were seen as the most crucial, dealing with young care-leaver's current circumstances and survival.

The research findings correspond to those from work done by adult academics over a longer period. There are different emphases and additions. For example, there was a concern for current circumstances, rather than an examination of supposed causal factors such as lack of preparation for leaving care, and experiences in care. Preparation was seen as very important, but the current circumstances of care leavers were seen to be of at least equal if not greater importance (see West 1997). The very different meanings of the term 'support' given by adult workers and young people were revealed through the research. Some academics noted that the emphasis on health was different. One way of looking at this correspondence is to congratulate adults for coming so close to young people's experience and research. This reinforced credibility, but a real test of participatory youth research will be whether findings will be taken up if they are different to the views of adults – a test of acceptance of young people's work, and of young people themselves.

Work with young people is never as straightforward as it can sound. A range of issues concerned with power relationships emerged during this piece of participatory research. The power relations of most interest were between adults and young people. Two sets of issues can be defined: first, research related, and, second, revolving around participation. Both offer insight into the broader social circumstances and general relationship between adults and young people. The second set of issues, regarding participation, has an obvious link to youth work, but the research issues also have a wider application to adults' work with young people and ideas of professionalism. The participation issues will have greater familiarity to many, and are only given in outline below. It is impossible to cover every point, however interesting, in detail here.[7]

Research issues

The major issues are interlinked, in particular the question of ownership of the project and the extent of training to be provided. These, in turn, are connected to the question of outcome, and whether the participatory research is to be merely an exercise in young people's participation or primarily a piece of research introducing new knowledge and/or perspectives on the world. Ownership of the research and of the project need to be separated.

Ownership of the research

Ownership of the research was experienced by both the young researchers and care leavers interviewed, as several explained on video (SCF/Loud Minority 1995). The process of establishing ownership produces a tension with ideas of research credibility and validity, especially challenging traditional academic perceptions. Issues of research credibility link back to nineteenth-century academic politics. To gain acceptance and recognition, the study of human society and social life (anthropology, sociology, psychology) was represented as objective and measurable, and, therefore, scientific. This framework is now contested on methodological grounds (idealised objectivity is impossible, and researchers have an effect through their presence), and in its value basis. Traditional research has seen young people as passive subjects, and been dominated by explanations of universal child development. Challenges to traditional research include a new paradigm of childhood. This recognises childhood and youth as culturally specific not global; as a variable of social analysis and experienced differently according to age, ethnicity, gender, class and so on; as not just a preparation for adulthood It also recognises that children and young people are generally a powerless and oppressed social group (Prout and James 1990).

A second aspect of credibility is that research must have some framework, philosophy and basis in order to work. The traditional emphasis on sampling, especially in quantitative research, and extrapolation from the few to the many, is a process which can ignore the circumstances and needs of minority populations. Research norms are enforced and reproduced by peers, institutions and bodies which govern careers and distribute funding. Norms have yet to be set for participatory research, and perhaps cannot be, since the process is important, the purpose being to contest hierarchies, in different circumstances. Research credibility is linked to the reputation of the staff and organisation conducting the work. Traditional research methods assist credibility for those working outside a university. For more challenging participatory research approaches, organisational credibility is important.

Ownership of the project

Ownership of the project concerns control over its direction and participants. This was only held by the young researchers to a limited extent, and involves the question of their participation at various levels of decision-making. For example, the project was financed by NatWest to a fixed figure, to be run by SCF, who allocated staff and local bases. The purpose of the project was to do research, and on the topic of leaving care. These were the major boundaries of the project.

An additional limit was time. Participatory processes generally require a lot of time and resources. Young people, especially those living in difficult circumstances, need support outside and alongside the project to enable their participation. The usual pace of adults' and agencies' work may be too fast (or too slow), especially at first, when unfamiliar territory is being explored by young people. The leaving-care project was completed rapidly (six months from recruitment of researchers to publication launch). This time limit was managerially created but extended at the young researchers' request. Time restrictions fuelled the work, creating an intensity and outcomes which might otherwise have been different. Project participants remain divided on the issue of time. If young people (or the adult research staff) had had easy opportunity to vary limits, the project might not have worked as well. The real underlying issue is not boundaries, but the importance of flexibility. Time is a good example of a process of joint inquiry, where tensions of agency and worker, adult and young person, aims and needs, have to be balanced.

The establishment of the project entailed SCF putting its reputation at risk (as it does in any work). Agency policy aims to circumvent risk. The basic ethical stance of SCF was conveyed to the researchers. Important issues were confidentiality, equal opportunities and child protection. Confidentiality was rapidly agreed, not least because of the young researchers' awareness of this issue through their own experience. The idea of equal opportunities provoked debate, initiated through a proposed section on the schedule indicating gender and ethnicity. At the heart of the complex debate was a general agreement valuing all humans. Therefore, it was asked why it was necessary to make differentiation. In addition, one young person's experience was of such information being used to exclude, ignore and harass, making it better not to be identified as Black. Here is an example of where discussion and final agreement was subtly influenced by adult knowledge and experience, in addition to agency values.

The discussion of child protection issues is an example of general and practical preparation for the young researchers about potential encounters, and dealing with difficult eventualities. Preparation included how to respond to requests for help (for money, for housing, for support, and so on), and how much to disclose about oneself. Staff from SCF projects were available to work with interviewees experiencing difficulties. This focus was establishing an ethical practice, involving the young researchers and making provision for the researched.

As these examples indicate, in the process of developing the research the balance between adults' intervention, their subtle influence, and young people's decision-making, is not finite, nor clearly demarcated. The important element is to maintain the ethos and principle of young people leading and taking decisions, and for adult practitioners always to question their intervention, and to reflect upon what they are saying and doing.

Credibility and validity

For research to have influence it needs to be credible. This is a political issue, regarding where norms and criteria governing research credibility originate, how they are maintained, and whether what is explained as rigour is inappropriate or exclusive rigidity. If young people's research is to be empowering, and go beyond simply gaining experience, their work must be believed and taken up. The basis of research credibility is the perception of the public, policy makers, academics and other professionals of its validity, generally expressed through evaluation of method. For the public such validity often depends on quantity. In this leaving-care research, a man calling a radio phone-in programme felt the research was not valid because huge numbers should have been interviewed. For other professionals, validity depends on detail of method, with some institutions biased towards quantitative or qualitative processes.

Such forms of validity depend on a research paradigm derived from the professional, constituted by training, peer review and defined processes. These may be alien to many groups of young people and other communities, where different forms and bases of knowledge exist, and/or where personal observation and experience presents a different reality and view of the world to that of the professional. Identities and perceptions are informed by age, gender, ethnicity, disability, sexuality, in addition to opportunities offered and constrained by class, income, housing, and so on.

For participatory research this produces a tension along a continuum between the professional, public and young people's perceptions and practice of research. One resulting pertinent issue is the question of training for young researchers: is it necessary before embarking on any research? If so, how much and what training is required? It is as well to remember that participatory projects generally involve groups who lack power, or are socially excluded and even vulnerable. Young people who attend sixth form college and university conduct research as part of their studies; young people who are homeless and unemployed do not, and if they are to do research, should they be trained in order to give the research credibility?

There are ethical and methodological issues involved here. Training young people from the outset in what is 'right' and 'wrong' in research aims and methods produces conceptual boundaries which constrain creative possibilities. For example, young care leavers did not experience their issues and problems as separate themes, but holistically. Their intensive discussions led to the production of a lengthy interview schedule, but this was not constrained by the need initially to categorise issues, nor by perceptions of length of interview, analysis, and so on. Training can defeat one of the purposes and benefits of undertaking participatory research. Training ultimately rests on a conception of research, knowledge and hierarchy, which means that the conventional research paradigm and researchers must be reproduced before the work is regarded as valid. Much depends on who owns the research; an agency using young people as insiders for access might have different perceptions to young people wanting to voice their circumstances through research.

Young people are also aware of issues of credibility and want their research to be valid. In the leaving-care research, the young people had assumed at the outset that they would use a questionnaire. This was a method with which they were familiar and felt was valid, rather than looking at innovatory techniques, such as drawings. They did take up the idea of open questions and so the interview became semi-structured, but choices and developments arose from a process of engagement and experiential work rather than training. The question of training is highlighted further by working with young people who neither read nor write. For example, in our participatory research with street children in Bangladesh (Khan 1997), lengthy training was inappropriate. Street children must earn their living and have limited time available for research. Learning research skills are less of a priority than reading and writing, so validity and rigour must be established in different ways. 'Training' comes through a process of informal education, particularly experiential, with adults (including professionals) and young people together developing an appropriate and valid method. This informal educational approach is at the heart of youth work. The greatest resource in solving project problems is the young people, who have ideas and knowledge of possibilities.

An alternative view is that training is appropriate because young people have rights to knowledge. This position rests to an extent on the notion of an objective reality, a dominant form of knowledge. The dilemma for workers is that while some empowerment might be offered through access to that knowledge, different realities and experiences can be suppressed. Informal and experiential education, starting from and respecting existing knowledge and perceptions, is a process of gaining information and understanding, and making decisions whether and how to use it, including challenging it.

Adults' attitudes

Training may assist but will not produce validity or credibility. The question of validity is political, just as children's rights and citizenship are contested and depend on dominant value bases and perceptions of the social order. Credibility in young people's research depends upon an acceptance that they are able to undertake research, and that their involvement is viable. There are research methods and practices which are generally not valid: for example, dishonest reporting in interviews, inventing the content of interviews. But some suggestions that young people's research cannot be valid derive from a belief that young people are not to be trusted, and will not tell the truth. This position of young people is similar to other communities who have been subject to outside research which has reached conclusions that are inappropriate or which disadvantage parts of the community, usually the less powerful such as women, children and poor people (Gill 1993).

The problem of adults' attitudes towards children, believing their research findings or accepting them as researchers, will not be overcome by training young people. The young care leavers' decision to interview staff brought them many frustrations. They found it difficult to find staff who would agree to be interviewed and take their research seriously. This particular test of participatory processes involves gatekeeping in reverse. For young people to gain access to staff, they must involve other sympathetic adults to request or invoke procedures on their behalf. In the leaving-care research, some assistance was given by SCF staff, but the problem was not taken up to its fullest extent. Apart from considerations of time (and funding, requiring a further residential for exploration and decision-making around the issue), taking action would have changed the nature of the research project. In addition, this process was a finding in itself: the difficulty of getting access to staff, and the flippancy with which some staff responded in the interview, contrasted with the broad professional statements supporting participation and empowerment of young people.

Researched to researchers

Through participation, young people acting as researchers do undertake some transformation, even without formal training. The nature of participatory research, involving people without power, generally means an experiential transition from being the researched to becoming researchers. For example, young people in care are used to being asked questions and, for many, leaving care brings a continuation of the experience, with form filling and interviews for benefits or training schemes. Change becomes evident through the research process as skills and ideas develop, yet the root issue for adult workers of when, where and if to intervene, and the nature of any intervention remains.

For example, the range of issues emerging through sharing experience and knowledge, meant the extent of possible research was considerable. The initial interview schedule developed by the young researchers was long – some fourteen pages. Clearly the interview would take time, and problems could arise through the interviewee becoming bored, tired, and refusing to complete. The interviewer also would require stamina. This was an adult's perception, leading to the dilemma of intervention: should the schedule be reduced? Possible difficulties were mentioned, but the young researchers went off to pilot the schedule. Most came to the next residential with the view that it was too long, and two were upset by having shown it to a student who had derided it as a research schedule. The plan was to reduce it but, on the young people's insistence that all issues were important, even with experience of piloting, the final version was even longer. Again, this produced dilemmas of intervention for adults: not taking action and 'allowing' the schedule to go ahead brought many worries for me: that interviews would not be completed, there would be no material and the young people and the agency would be let down. Such fears resulted from an adult perception, based on 'knowing best'. In fact, the interviews were completed, the material was good, and demonstrated other benefits of participatory research – the young people were able to work with other young people to complete an extensive schedule in a way certainly not possible by adults.

Calculating a leaving-care grant provided another dilemma. The young researchers insisted on second-hand goods and low estimates for new goods, and although the total was greater than currently paid, the recommended amount could have been much more. This was a case of respecting an informed and very realistic decision by young people, rather than insisting on a different calculation basis.

Participation issues

A range of issues around participation emerged, especially around relationships, roles and power. These partly derive from the way participatory projects are established. For any particular project the decision to have participation is made by the powerful – adults. Young people are recruited, but the process of selection provides the first group of young people who can make decisions about the project alongside, or for, adults. For example, young people in the leaving-care project wanted to take part in all decision-making. They disliked the residential site (this proved difficult to change): they wanted to, and did, organise, facilitate and chair sessions at the residential and take places on the steering group; not all wanted to take part and show their faces in the video (some having bad experiences of the media). Important elements were managing the practicalities of what was possible, funding available and its purpose, processes of daily participation, and meeting research aims and credibility.

Another point of importance concerns expectations and outcomes. Empowerment offers opportunities and enthusiasm for change: the young researchers were keen their work should have impact and influence. This meant that the project did not end when the research was completed, but many young people continued to disseminate findings afterwards (West 1996c). There are two issues here: expectations and responsibility. Influence is hard to achieve, difficult to measure, and change is not always immediate or visible. Expectations need to be realistic, but also not dampen enthusiasm or create the feeling that nothing can change.

Responsibility for achieving change lies not only with the young people themselves. The research highlights their needs and experiences, but their lives do not have to be devoted to promoting change. Adults in general, and youth workers in particular, have responsibility to look at their own attitudes, behaviour and work in the light of young people's experience, and take action to achieve change. This may involve recognition that some cherished practices and priorities need to be altered.

Conclusion

Participatory research led by young people provides a good example of the tensions which mark their relationship with adults. Issues include notions of competence and trust, dominant paradigms of knowledge and validity, detail of everyday practice in the location of power, the availability of time and access to resources. Youth work values of empowerment and participation can challenge such models and practices, but require continuous reflection on the process of engagement in order to be fulfilled. The best resource available ultimately is the young people themselves. Participatory research gives the opportunity for young people's circumstances, needs and experiences to be validated and voiced: a process involving their development, but learning for all of us.

Notes

1 'South' is used in preference to 'third world'.
2 Participatory research in the South began in rural areas, aiming for rapid completion, and is known as PRA – Participatory Rapid Appraisal, or Participatory Rural Appraisal, or RRA – Rapid Rural Appraisal (see Chambers 1994 for an exposition of the differences).
3 I acknowledge Claire Hackett in formulating the question 'what exactly is participatory research?', with whom I ran a seminar on participatory research in Belfast in 1996.
4 Being in care is officially being 'looked after by the local authority', but young people I have worked with prefer the term 'in care', seeing it as satirical.
5 SCF is organised in regional and country programmes around the world, including work in the UK.
6 The projects were BYPASS (Bolton Young People's Advice and Support Services), Care and Justice Yorkshire, Leeds Children's Rights Service, Kensington and Chelsea Leaving Care and LifeChance. Most operate in partnership with the local authority.
7 Questions of payment to interviewees and young researchers are not discussed.

Bibliography

Biehal, N., Clayden, J., Stein, M. and Wade, J. (1995) *Moving On: Young People and Leaving Care Schemes*, London: HMSO.

BSA (British Sociological Association) (n.d.) *Statement of Ethical Practice and Guidelines for Good Professional Conduct*, London: British Sociological Association.

Chambers, R. (1994) 'Participatory Rural Appraisal (PRA): Challenges, Potentials and Paradigm', *World Development* 22(10): 1437–54.

Cornwall, A. and Jewkes, R. (1995) 'What is participatory research?' *Social Science and Medicine* 41(12): 1667–76.

Everitt, A. and Gibson, A. (1994) *Making it Work: Researching in the Voluntary Sector*, London: HMSO.

Everitt, A., Hardiker, P., Littlewood, J. and Mullender, A. (1992) *Applied Research for Better Practice*, Basingstoke: Macmillan.

Fook, J. (ed.) (1996) *The Reflective Researcher: Social Workers' Theories of Practice Research*, St Leonards, Australia: Allen and Unwin.

Garnett, L. (1992) *Leaving Care and After*, London: National Children's Bureau.

Gill, G. (1993) *O.K., the Data's Lousy, but its all we've got (being a critique of conventional methods)*, London: International Institute for Environment and Development, Gatekeeper Series no. 38.

Gleed, S. 1996 'A first attempt at research: surveying rural social work practice', in J. Fook (ed.) (1996) *The Reflective Researcher: Social Workers' Theories of Practice Research*, St Leonards, Australia: Allen and Unwin.

Gordon, S. (n.d.) *Balancing Acts: How to Encourage Youth Participation*, Leicester: National Youth Bureau.

Hackett, C., Keenan, P., Connolly, M. *et al.* (1996) *Out of our Mouths not out of our Heads: A report of drugs and drug use in West Belfast compiled by and for young people*, Belfast: West Belfast Economic Forum/Save the Children.

Hart, E. and Bond, M. (1995) *Action Research for Health and Social Care*, Buckingham: Open University Press.

Hart, R. (1992) *Children's Participation: From Tokenism to Citizenship*, Florence, Italy: UNICEF International Child Development Centre.

Homan, R. (1991) *The Ethics of Social Research*, Harlow: Longman.

HMSO (1960) *The Youth Service in England and Wales* (Albemarle Report), London: HMSO.

—— (1982) *Experience and Participation: Report of the Review Group on the Youth Service in England* (Thompson Report) London: HMSO.

Joyce, G. (n.d.) *Taking the Wraps off Participation*, Leicester: Youth Clubs UK.

Khan, S. (1997) *Street Children's Research*, Bangladesh, Dhaka: Save the Children .

Lacey, F. (1987) 'Youth workers as community workers', in T. Jeffs and M. Smith (eds) *Youth Work*, Basingstoke: Macmillan.

Munday, C. 1996 'Voices: a peer research approach to needs assessment', *Young People Now* 28–9 August.

Nevison, C. (1997) *A Matter of Opinion*, Newcastle: Save the Children.

Prout, A. and James, A. (1990) 'A new paradigm for the sociology of childhood? Provenance, promise and problems', in A. James and A. Prout (eds) *Constructing and Reconstructing Childhood*, Basingstoke: Falmer Press.

Reason, P. (ed.) (1994) *Participation in Human Inquiry*, London: Sage.

Rosseter, B. (1987) 'Youth workers as educators', in T. Jeffs and M. Smith (eds) *Youth Work*, Basingstoke: Macmillan.

Save the Children Fund/Loud Minority (1995) *Does Anyone Care?*, video.

Smith, M. (1980) *Creators not Consumers: Rediscovering Social Education*, Leicester: National Association of Youth Clubs.

—— (1988) *Developing Youth Work*, Milton Keynes: Open University Press.

Stein, M. and Carey, K. (1986) *Leaving Care*, Oxford: Basil Blackwell.

Stanley, L. (ed.) (1990) 'Feminist Praxis: Research, Theory and Epistemology', in L. Stanley (ed.) *Feminist Sociology*, London: Routledge.

Treseder, P. (1997) *Empowering Children and Young People: a training manual*, London: Children's Rights Office/Save the Children.

Waldman, J. and Hague, F. (1996) 'Modelling mutality', *Young People Now* 28–9 September.

West, A. (1996a) 'Young people, participatory research and experiences of leaving care', *PLA Notes: Notes on Participatory Learning and Action* 25: 73–6.

—— (1996b) *But What Is It...? A Critique of Undefined Participation*, Leeds: Save the Children.

—— (1996c) 'Rights not Rhetoric', *Community Care Inside* 26 September–2 October: 8.

—— (1997) 'Different questions, different ideas: child-led research and other participation', paper given at 'Children's participation in research and programming workshops', Universities of London and Sussex.

West, A., Costello, E., Manning, E. *et al.* (1995) *You're On Your Own: young people's research on leaving care*, London: Save the Children.

Whyte, W.F. (ed.) (1991) *Participatory Action Research*, New York: Sage.

INDEX

200